# HOW SOFTWARE IS BUILT

# {QUALITY SOFTWARE}

## by

Gerald M. Weinberg

\* \* \* \* \*

PUBLISHED BY:

Weinberg & Weinberg

How Software Is Built

(Quality Software Series Volume 1)

Copyright © 2014 by Gerald M. Weinberg

# Table of Contents

Patterns

**WHAT TO READ NEXT?**

**BOOKS FOR CONSULTANTS (AND OTHERS)**

**THE QUALITY SOFTWARE SERIES**

**THE SYSTEMS THINKING SERIES**

**TECHNOLOGY/PSYCHOLOGY**

**NOVELS: TECHNOLOGY LESSONS FRAMED IN FICTION ABOUT WOMEN OF POWER.**

**SHORT FICTION: FUN LITTLE LESSONS.**

# New Preface

*"Teachers not only teach, but they also learn." - Sauk saying*

This book is a kind of an Anniversary present, commemorating my now-50-year love affair with computers. In the 40 years since I first sat at my computer to write down what I had learned in my first 40 years in the computer business, I've learned an enormous amount. Much of it has been written in the second, third, and fourth volumes of *Software Quality Management*. Some has been written in a variety of other books and articles, including, *Amplifying Your Effectiveness* (edited with Naomi Karten and James Bach), *What Did You Say? : The Art of Giving and Receiving Feedback* (with Edie and Charlie Seashore; *Perfect Software--and Other Illusions About Testing*; the *Roundtable on Project Management* and the *Roundtable on Technical Leadership* (both edited with Jim Bullock, and Marie Benesh); *Weinberg on Writing: The Fieldstone Method*; and *More Secrets of Consulting: The Consultant's Self-Esteem Tool Kit*.

There are also my novels, including, so far, the *Aremac* series, the *Stringers* series, *Earth's Endless Effort*, *Mistress of Molecules*,

*Freshman Murders*, and *The Hands of God*–each of which attempts to bring lessons to the reader through the medium of compelling stories of adventure. And one of the major reasons I've been writing novels and in other formats is what I've learned from reader feedback.

Typical of this learning when I read a book review written by my good friend, Dan Starr. About somebody else's book, he wrote, "This book is a gold mine." The next time I saw him, I asked him why he never called one of *my* books a gold mine.

"You know what a gold mine is like," he replied. "There are a few gold nuggets, but you have to sift through tons of worthless tailings to find them."

I was starting to feel better, but then he added, "Your books are more like coal mines."

"Oh?" was all I could muster.

"Yes. You know what a coal mine is like. Every shovelful contains something worthwhile. Every one."

I'm satisfied to be writing coal mines. Oh, sure, I once imagined that I could write a book in which every sentence, every word, would be 24-karat gold, but *nobody* can sustain that level for an entire book. Even the "Greatest Book Ever Written" has long boring, repetitive passages that not even the most ardent evangelist will ever quote. So, if even God won't write a solid gold book, I'm content to drop that particular fantasy.

But, readers tell me that compared with lots of other books, my books are dense, dense, reading. A common complaint about the Quality Software Management Series is this: "They're just too expensive and too big to take in all at once." So, when Volume I went out of print for a while (they're also expensive to print), I took another look and decided to break it into smaller, less expensive volumes.

I also learned that for many potential readers outside of the United States, simply paying the shipping for one of those volumes more than doubled the cost–in American dollars, no less. So, to make them available to non-Americans (and some Americans, too), I've chosen to make eBook versions, as well.

I've also learned that much of the "heaviness" of those volumes came from all the scholarly material, such as footnotes and references. Nowadays, with search engines on the internet, readers who wish to follow up on something they read don't really need those references. By omitting them, I make the volumes lighter, and shorter. And friendlier to the average modern reader.

The principal contents, on the other hand, are largely unchanged. I was writing about general principles–illustrated by specific examples–much of which derived from my *Introduction to General Systems Thinking* and *General Principles of System Design* (with Dani Weinberg). There are, of course, new examples from the Internet Age, but the fundamental principles remain the

3

same.

For the modern reader, I suggest they add *Practice* problems based on their more recent experiences. For me to add such examples throughout would be such an overwhelming task it would delay the books by a number of years. And that's one more thing I hear from my readers: " "Get the books out there for us. Don't delay!"

One more explanation. I've taken the word "management" out of the title, leaving, simply, "Quality Software." Why? Because too many people who should be reading this material interpreted "management" to mean "managers." Certainly these books are for managers, but they're also for everyone else in the business of producing quality software.

I've learned anew that most of the improvements in our business do not come from managers, but from underneath. As many have said, "Change always comes from the bottom. Nobody holding four Aces has ever asked for a new deal." And that's why I'm hoping that these format changes will empower everybody to create a new deal in software.

# Preface

*"Poor management can increase software costs more*

*rapidly than any other factor." - Barry Boehm*

This book is a kind of an Anniversary present, commemorating my 40-year love affair with computers. Early in 1950, I read a *Time* magazine cover story about computers, or "Thinking Machines." The cover itself was by Time's favorite cover artist, Artzybashef. It depicted an anthropomorphic electronic box with an eye looking at a paper tape held in its right hand while its left hand typed some output on a teletype. The box was topped with a Navy cap with lots of "scrambled eggs," and the caption read, "Mark III. Can man build a superman?"

A bit sensational, yes, but it made a profound impression on a 16-year-old about to graduate from high school. I may not recall many details of the article, but I clearly recall that I decided on the spot computers would be my life.

One of the facts that impressed me in the article was that IBM was a big factor in the business of building computing machines. In 1956, when I was unable to find a university that taught about computers, I went to work for IBM.

For 13 years, I took IBM seriously, especially the THINK part. IBM was right. Thinking was essential. But after a while I noticed that IBM and its customers often honored thinking, but didn't practice it. Especially in the software side of the business, which always seemed to take last place in the hearts of IBM executives.

As far as I could tell, little THINK signs on each desk never helped us get software out the door. Yet IBM managers never seemed to do much else to help the process. Later, after I left IBM for an independent consulting career, I learned that IBM's managers were no different from the rest.

All over the world, software managers gave lip service to thinking, but didn't do much about it. For one thing, they never understood the reasons that people didn't think when they ought to. Of course, I didn't understand either.

Looking back, I realize why the *Time* article had so impressed me. In school, everyone told me how smart I was. True, I did outstanding work on all sorts of tests, but I never seemed to be able to think effectively about my own life. I was a miserable kid, and I thought that "thinking machines" might help me solve my problems.

Well, "thinking machines" didn't solve my problems—they made them worse. When I tried to build software, the computer unfailingly accentuated all my mistakes. When I didn't think right about a program, the program bombed. The computer, I learned, was a *mirror* of my intelligence, and I wasn't too impressed by my reflection.

Later, when I wrote larger programs in concert with other people, I learned that the computer was not just a mirror, but a *magnifying* mirror. Any time we didn't think straight about our software project, we made a colossal monster. I began to learn that if we were ever to make good use of "thinking machines," we would have to start by improving our own thinking.

I began to study thinking as a subject in itself, particularly thinking as applied to software problems. Through the generosity of IBM, I went back to school and wrote a thesis on using computers as tools to mirror our minds. I travelled all over the world, visiting software organizations and studying how they think —about software. I shared ideas with people, and tried to put those ideas in practice on software projects. I observed what worked and what didn't—and I revised my ideas. I published some of them and then used feedback from hundreds of readers to refine them. This book summarizes what I have learned up to now about managing software projects effectively.

Why is managing software projects so important? One of the predictions in that ancient *Time* article was the following:

Around each working computer hover young mathematicians with dreamy eyes. On desks flecked with frothy figures, they translate real-life problems into figure-language. It usually takes them much longer to prepare a problem than it takes the machine to solve it.

These human question-answerers are sure to lag farther and farther behind the question-answering machines.

Not all of the predictions in the article came true (up until now), but this one certain did. Since that day when I became one of those dreamy-eyed young "question-answerers" (the word "programmer" hadn't yet been coined), I have learned that there are three fundamental abilities you need if you're not to lag farther and farther behind:

1. the ability to observe what's happening and to understand the significance of your observations

2. the ability to act congruently in difficult interpersonal situations, even though you may be confused, or angry, or so afraid you want to run away and hide

3. the ability to understand complex situations so you can plan a project and then observe and act so as to keep the project going according to plan, or modify the plan.

All three abilities are essential for quality software management, but I don't want to write a large, imposing book. Therefore, like any good software manager, I've decomposed the project into three smaller projects, each one addressing one of these three fundamental abilities. For reasons that will become clearer in the book, I am starting with the third ability—*the ability to understand complex situations*.

In other words, this is a *think* book. Its motto is the same as IBM's, because it's my way of paying back IBM and others for the wonderful things I've received from 40 years in the software business.  I can imagine no finer gift than helping someone, as others have helped me, to think more effectively about a subject that is so important to them personally, as well as to the world.

*****

# Part I Patterns Of Quality

In the midst of a struggle over software quality, it sometimes seems that producing and maintaining software is a random series of events. In a time of chaotic overload, that's a comforting idea. If the events are truly random, then you need not waste time thinking about what you should do. Just keep struggling as hard and as long as you can, so nobody can blame you for failure.

But if you sit back and reflect for a moment, you'll notice that producing and maintaining software is *not* a random series of events. There are patterns, and these patterns offer an opportunity to take control of our products, our organizations, and our lives.

In case your own life in the software industry has been too frantic for you to notice, we'll use our first few chapters to explore the concept of cultural patterns, introduce the major cultural patterns in software, and examine what's necessary to move from one pattern to another.

# Chapter 1: What Is Quality? Why Is It Important?

*"You can fool all of the people some of the time, and some of the people all of the time, but you can't fool all of the people all of the time."- Abraham Lincoln*

People in the software business put great stress on removing ambiguity, and so do writers. But sometimes writers are intentionally ambiguous, as in the title of this book. "Quality Software Management" means both "the management of quality software" and "quality management in the software business," because I believe that the two are inseparable. Both meanings turn on the word "quality," so if we are to keep the ambiguity within reasonable bounds, we first need to address the meaning of that often misunderstood term.

## 1.1 A Tale Of Software Quality

My sister's daughter, Terra, is the only one in the family who has followed Uncle Jerry in the writer's trade. She writes fascinating books on the history of medicine, and I follow each one's progress as if it were one of my own. For that reason, I was terribly distressed when her first book, *Disease in the Popular*

10

*American Press*, came out with a number of gross typographical errors in which whole segments of text disappeared (see Figure 1-1). I was even more distressed to discover that those errors were caused by an error in the word processing software she used—CozyWrite, published by one of my clients, the MiniCozy Software Company.

*The next day, too, the Times printed a letter from "Medicus," objecting to the misleading implication in the microbe story that diphtheria could ever be inoculated against; the writer flatly asserted that there would never be a vaccine for this disease because, unlike smallpox, diphtheria re-*

*Because Times articles never included proof—never told how people knew what they claimed—the uninformed reader had no way to distinguish one claim from another.*

**Figure 1-1. Part of a sample page from Terra Ziporyn's book showing how the CozyWrite word processor lost text after "re-" in Terra's book.**

Terra asked me to discuss the matter with MiniCozy on my next visit. I located the project manager for CozyWrite, and he acknowledged the existence of the error.

"It's a rare bug," he said.

"I wouldn't say so," I countered. "I found over twenty-five instances in her book."

"But it would only happen in a book-sized project. Out of over 100,000 customers, we probably didn't have 10 who undertook a project of that size as a single file."

"But my niece noticed. It was her first book, and she was devastated."

"Naturally I'm sorry for her, but it wouldn't have made any sense for us to try to fix the bug for 10 customers."

"Why not? You advertise that CozyWrite handles book-sized projects."

"We tried to do that, but the features didn't work. Eventually, we'll probably fix them, but for now, chances are we would introduce a worse bug—one that would affect hundreds or thousands of customers. I believe we did the right thing."

As I listened to this project manager, I found myself caught in an emotional trap. As software consultant to MiniCozy, I had to agree, but as uncle to an author, I was violently opposed to his line of reasoning. If someone at that moment had asked me, "Is CozyWrite a quality product?" I would have been tongue-tied.

How would you have answered?

## 1.2 The Relativity of Quality

The reason for my dilemma lies in the *relativity of quality*. As the MiniCozy story crisply illustrates, what is adequate quality to one person may be inadequate quality to another.

### *1.2.1. Finding the relativity*

If you examine various definitions of quality, you will always find this relativity. You may have to examine with care, though, for the relativity is often hidden, or at best, implicit.

Take for example Crosby's definition:

*"Quality is meeting requirements."*

Unless your requirements come directly from heaven (as some developers seem to think), a more precise statement would be:

*"Quality is meeting **some person's** requirements."*

For each different person, the same product will generally have different "quality," as in the case of my niece's word processor. My MiniCozy dilemma is resolved once I recognize that

a. To Terra, the people involved were her readers.

b. To MiniCozy's project manager, the people involved were (the majority of) his customers.

### 1.2.2 Who was that masked man?

In short, quality does not exist in a non-human vacuum.

***Every statement about quality is a statement about some person(s).***

That statement may be explicit or implicit. Most often, the "who" is implicit, and statements about quality sound like something Moses brought down from Mount Sinai on a stone tablet. That's why so many discussions of software quality are unproductive: It's my stone tablet versus your Golden Calf.

When we encompass the relativity of quality, we have a tool

to make those discussions more fruitful. Each time somebody asserts a definition of software quality, we simply ask,

*"Who is the person behind that statement about quality."*

Using this heuristic, let's consider a few familiar but often conflicting ideas about what constitutes software quality:

a. "Zero defects is high quality."

1. to a user such as a surgeon whose work would be disturbed by those defects

2. to a manager who would be criticized for those defects

b. "Lots of features is high quality."

1. to users whose work can use those features—if they know about them

2. to marketers who believe that features sell products

c. "Elegant coding is high quality."

1. to developers who place a high value on the opinions of their peers

2. to professors of computer science who enjoy elegance

d. "High performance is high quality."

1. to users whose work taxes the capacity of their machines

2. to salespeople who have to submit their products to benchmarks

e. "Low development cost is high quality."

1. to customers who wish to buy thousands of copies of the

software

2. to project managers who are on tight budgets

f. "Rapid development is high quality."

1. to users whose work is waiting for the software

2. to marketers who want to colonize a market before the competitors can get in

g. "User-friendliness is high quality."

1. to users who spend 8 hours a day sitting in front of a screen using the software

2. to users who can't remember interface details from one use to the next

### 1.2.3 The political dilemma

Recognizing the relativity of quality often resolves the *semantic* dilemma. At the start of a book on quality, this is a monumental contribution, but it still does not resolve the *political* dilemma:

*More quality for one person may mean less quality for another.*

For instance, if our goal were "total quality," we'd have to do a summation over *all* relevant people. Thus, this "total quality" effort would have to *start* with a comprehensive requirements process that identifies and involves all relevant people. Then, for each design, for each software engineering approach, we would have to assign a quality measure for each person. Summing these measures would then yield the total quality for each different approach.

In practice, of course, no software development project ever uses such an elaborate process. Instead, most people are eliminated by a prior process that decides:

*Whose opinion of quality is to count when making decisions?*

For instance, the project manager at MiniCozy decided, without hearing arguments from Terra, that her opinion carried minuscule weight in his "software engineering" decision. From this case, we see that software engineering is *not* a democratic business. Nor, unfortunately, is it a *rational* business, for these decisions about "who counts" are generally made on an emotional basis.

## 1.3 Quality Is Value To Some Person

The political/emotional dimension of quality is made evident by a somewhat different definition of quality. The idea of "requirements" is a bit too innocent to be useful in this early stage, because it says nothing about *whose* requirements count the most. A more workable definition would be this:

*"Quality is value to some person."*

By "value," I mean, "What are people willing to pay (do) to have their requirements met." Suppose, for instance, that Terra

16

were not *my* niece, but the niece of the president of the MiniCozy Software Company. Knowing MiniCozy's president's reputation for impulsive emotional action, the project manager might have defined "quality" of the word processor differently. In that case, Terra's opinion would have been given high weight in the decision about which faults to repair.

In short, the definition of "quality" is always *political* and *emotional*, because it always involves a series of decisions about whose opinions count, and how much they count relative to one another. Of course, much of the time these political/emotional decisions—like all important political/emotional decisions—are hidden from public view. Most of us software people like to appear rational. That's why very few people appreciate the power of this definition of quality. Hopefully, its power will be revealed throughout these volumes.

What makes our task even more difficult is that most of the time these decisions are hidden even from the conscious minds of the persons who make them. That's why one of the most important actions of a quality manager is to bring such decisions into consciousness, if not always into public awareness. That will be one of our major tasks.

## 1.4 Another Story About Quality

To test our understanding of this definition, as well as its applicability, let's read another story:

One of the favorite pastimes of my youth was playing cribbage with my father. Cribbage is a card game, invented by the poet Sir John Suckling, very popular in some regions of the world, but essentially unknown in others. After my father died, I missed playing cribbage with him and was hard pressed to find a regular partner. Consequently, I was delighted to discover a shareware cribbage program for the Macintosh, "Precision Cribbage" by Doug Brent, of San Jose, CA.

Precision Cribbage was a rather nicely engineered piece of software, I thought, especially when compared with the great majority of shareware. I was especially pleased to find that it gave me a good game, but wasn't good enough to beat me more than 1 or 2 games out of 10. Therefore, I sent Doug the requested postcard from my home town as a shareware fee and played many happy games.

After a while, though, I discovered two clear errors in the scoring algorithm of Precision Cribbage. One was an intermittent failure to count correctly hands with three cards of one denomination and two of another (a "full house," in poker terminology). This was clearly an unintentional flaw, because sometimes such hands were counted correctly.

The second error, however, may have been a misunderstanding of the scoring rules (which were certainly part of the "requirements" for a program that purported to play a card game). It had to do with counting hands that had three cards of the same suit when a fourth card of that suit was cut. In this case, I could actually *prove* mathematically that the algorithm was incorrect.

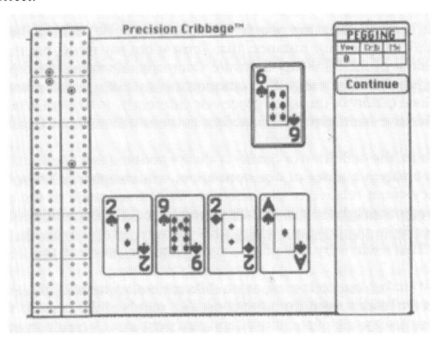

**Figure 1-2. An example of a miscounted cribbage hand. The correct score should be 4, not 8.**

What makes this story relevant is that even with two scoring errors in the game, I was sufficiently satisfied with the quality of Precision Cribbage to

a. keep on playing it, for at least several of my valuable hours each week

19

b. pay the shareware "fee," even though I could have omitted payment with no fear of retribution of any kind

In short, Precision Cribbage had great value to me, value which I was willing and able to demonstrate by spending my own time and (if requested) money. Moreover, Doug's correction of these errors would have added very little to the value of the software.

## 1.5. Why Improving Quality Is So Difficult

The tale of Precision Cribbage demonstrates that "meeting requirements" is not an adequate definition of quality, unless you're willing to accept a most unconventional definition of "requirements." It also demonstrates the inadequacy of definitions of quality based on errors, such as,

*"Quality is the absence of error."*

Such definitions are easy to refute, yet they have dominated thinking about quality software for many years. This makes it easy for software developers and managers to ignore requests to "improve software quality." But don't they want to improve quality, even if nobody else was asking for it, just to satisfy their own pride? Of course they do, but nothing happens. Why not?

### 1.5.1. *"It's not too bad."*

The stories of CosyWrite and Precision Cribbage are typical of hundreds of cases I could cite, and you could undoubtedly

20

supply many examples of your own. If you asked the developers, "Are you interested in a high-quality product?" I'm sure their professional pride would supply the answer, "Of course!"

But suppose you asked specifically about improving CosyWrite or Precision Cribbage. They would reply, "But it already *is* a good quality product. Of course it has bugs, but *all* software has bugs. Besides, it's better than the competition." And, of course, all three of these statements are provably correct:

a. People are using their product, and are happy with it, so it is "good quality."

b. All software does have bugs. At least we can't prove otherwise.

c. People buy it over the competition, so it must be better, in their opinion.

Under the circumstances, there's very little motivation to improve the quality unless pushed from outside. If people stop using their product, or buying it, then the developers might decide to "improve quality," but by then it will probably be too late. Organizations that sell software simply fade away when faced with a competitor that operates in a more effective manner.

Organizations that produce software internally for larger organizations have little competition, so they simply stagnate. Whether or not their stagnation matters depends on what their parent organization defines as "quality." If the parent gets the value they need, and don't know any better, then the stagnation continues. Once they become dissatisfied, however, a crisis begins.

### 1.5.2. "It's not possible."

Did you know that if you were 8'6" tall you could get a job as a starting center in the NBA and earn $5,000,000 a year? Now that you know that, why aren't you starting on a growth program? It's a silly question, because you don't know *how* to grow several feet taller.

Did you know that by reducing the faults in your software to less than 1 in a million lines of code you could increase your market by $5,000,000 a year? Now that you know that, why aren't you starting on a quality program? It's a silly question, because you don't know *how* to reduce software faults to less than 1 in a million lines of code.

Phil Crosby, in *Quality is Free*, says that the motivation for improving quality always starts with a study of the "cost of quality." (I would prefer the term, "value of quality," but it's the same idea.) In my consulting, I frequently talk to managers who seem obsessed with cutting the cost of software, or reducing development time, but I seldom find a manager obsessed with improving quality. It's easy for them to tell me what it's worth to cut costs or expedite a schedule, but the value of improved quality seems to be something they've never thought of measuring.

Yet when I suggest measuring the value of quality, they often respond as if I told them to measure the value of growing to 8' 6". Why bother measuring the value of something that you don't have the slightest idea how to achieve? And why try to achieve something whose value you don't appreciate? Figure 1-3 shows this vicious cycle in the form of a "diagram of effects," a form of diagram we will explain later and use throughout this volume. For now, lets just concentrate on what it says about why improving quality is so difficult.

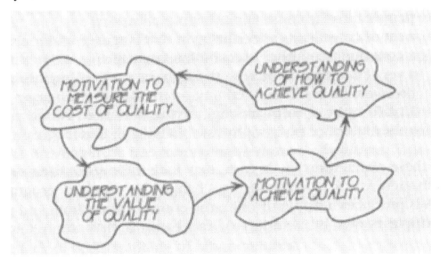

**Figure 1-3. A vicious cycle that prevents organizations from starting to improve quality.**

The diagram of Figure 1-3 can be read optimistically or pessimistically. Optimistically, it says that once an organization begins to understand the true value of quality, its motivation to improve will rise, which while drive its understanding of how to improve, which will in turn lead to a better understanding of the value of quality. That's why Crosby likes to start organizational change with a "cost of quality" study.

Pessimistically, though, the cycle can be seen as inhibiting a change to higher quality. If there is no understanding of the value of quality, then there is no motivation to achieve quality, and thus no improvement in the understanding of how to achieve quality. And without knowing how to achieve quality, why would anyone try to measure its value?

### 1.5.3. The lock-on

Figure 1-3 happens to be a simple example of a "lock-on" effect. A locked-on system tends to hold itself to an existing pattern, even against "logical" reasons to change. An excellent example of a lock-on is the choice of a standard programming language. Once an organization is using a single programming language—for whatever historical reasons—the cost of changing increases, the motivation to study the value of other alternatives decreases, and the knowledge of how to obtain those alternatives disappears. As a result, the organization "locks on" to the language, just as a country locks on to the side of the road used for driving.

In this volume, we'll see many examples of lock-on situations, but for now we simply want to not that lock-ons occur in clusters. When you lock on to a particular programming language, you also tend to lock on to some or all of the following:

1. a set of software tools supporting that language

2. hardware systems that support a particular dialect of that language

3. people trained in particular schools

4. people hired from certain other organizations

5. a set of consultants specializing in that language and tools

6. a community of other users of that language

7. a set of managers who rose through the ranks using this language

8. professional books and training oriented to that language

9. a philosophy of software engineering associated with that language

10. a user interface philosophy associated with that language

Each of these characteristics, in turn, may lock the organization onto another set of characteristics. Attempting to change the standard programming language thus produces a ripple through the entire organization, and each furrow of this ripple is met by a variety of mechanisms that attempt to prevent a change.

It doesn't matter that changing the language would be "good" for the organization. As Virginia Satir, the family therapist, used to say

> *"People will always choose the familia0r over the comfortable."*

### 1.6. Software Culture and Subcultures

All these interrelated lock-ons produce patterns. Every time Dani (my anthropologist partner) and I arrive at a new organization to consult on managing software organizations, we quickly notice two essential facts:

1. No two software organizations are exactly alike.

2. No two software organizations are entirely different.

Because of (1), it's not possible to have off-the-rack solutions to really important problems of software management, but because of (2), we don't have to start over from scratch with every new organization. There are commonalties from one software organization to another, even though they are different sizes, in different industries, working with different programming languages, in different countries, and even in different decades. This book is very much concerned with those commonalties.

A rather anthropological way of expressing this observation is that there is some sort of "software culture" that transcends boundaries of time, space, and circumstance. There are a number of ways to verify the existence of this "software culture." For one thing, software books sell very well in English all over the world. The software culture is very much an English-language culture.

The books also sell well in translation, and the same software jokes —like Levine, the genius tailor—are funny all over the world for decades. Software meetings are international, and surveys of attendees show that they cross industries and age groups as well. We are fortunate that such a software culture exists, for it allows us to learn from one another. Thus, any truths that we have learned with our clients should have potential value for you and your organization.

One of the things most valuable truths we have learned is that the overall software culture seems to come in a few different patterns—clusters of characteristics they have in common. One way of distinguishing these patterns is to observe *the quality of the software they produce*. We have come to believe that software organizations lock on to a particular level of quality, and that change is prevented by the "conservative nature of culture." This conservatism is manifested primarily in

a. the satisfaction with their current level of quality

b. the fear of losing that level in an attempt to do even better

c. the lack of understanding of other cultures

d. the invisibility of their own culture

Quality is important because quality is value. The ability to control quality is the ability to control the value of your software efforts. To reach a new culture of quality software, developers and managers must learn to deal effectively with these factors. That is the subject of this book.

## 1.7. Helpful Hints and Suggestions

• Of course you can't do a perfect job of identifying all potential users of your software and determining what they value, but that doesn't mean you won't benefit from trying. In fact, you'll probably find it beneficial just to try doing it in your head. Once you've experienced those benefits, you may decide to interview at least a few major users to find out where their values lie.

• Because of the conservative nature of culture, attempts to change are always met with "resistance." You will be better able to cope with such "resistance" if you recognize it as attempts to preserve what is good about the old way of doing things. Even better will be to begin a change project by acknowledging the value of the old way, and determining which characteristics you wish to preserve, even though changing the cultural pattern.

## 1.8. Summary

1. Quality is relative. What is quality to one person may even be lack of quality to another.

2. Finding the relativity involves detecting the implicit person or persons in the statement about quality, by asking, "Who is the person behind that statement about quality."

3. Quality is neither more nor less than value to some person

or persons. This view allows us to reconcile such statements as,*"Zero defects is high quality."* , *"Lots of features is high quality."* , *"Elegant coding is high quality."* , *"High performance is high quality."* , *"Low development cost is high quality."* , *"Rapid development is high quality."* , *"User-friendliness is high quality."* All of the statements can be true at the same time.

4. Quality is almost always a political/emotional issue, though we like to pretend it can be settled rationally.

5. Quality is not identical with freedom from errors. A software product that does not even conform to its formal requirements could be considered of high quality by some of its users.

6. Improving quality is so difficult because organizations tend to lock on to a specific pattern of doing things. They adapt to the present level of quality, they don't know what is needed to change to new level, and they don't really try to find out.

7. The patterns adopted by software organizations tend to fall into a few clusters, or subcultures, each of which produces characteristic results.

8. Cultures are inherently conservative. This conservatism is manifested primarily in

    a. the satisfaction with a particular level of quality

    b. the fear of losing that level in an attempt to do even

better

    c. the lack of understanding of other cultures

    d. the invisibility of their own culture

**1.9. Practice**

1. I wrote to Doug Brent, telling him how grateful I was and showing him the two erroneous cases, but haven't gotten a reply so far. I wouldn't mind if Precision Cribbage were corrected, but I wouldn't pay very much for the corrections, because their value was reduced once I had an approximate cribbage program with which to play. Discuss how the value, and thus the definition of quality, changes for a particular software product over time, as early versions of the product, or competing products, come into use.

2. Produce a list of characteristics that an organization might lock onto when standardizing on a given hardware architecture.

3. What evidence can you produce to indicate that people in your organization are indeed satisfied with the level of quality they produce? How does the organization deal with people who express dissatisfaction with that level?

# Chapter 2. Software Subcultures

*"I have had discussion with executives in hundreds of different businesses and industries. Regardless of the nation, product, service, or group I am never disappointed. Someone always says: 'You have to recognize that our business is different.' Because they usually see only their business, they never realize how alike businesses are. Certainly the technology and the methods of distribution can be very different. But the people involved—their motivations and reactions—are the same." - Philip B. Crosby*

What Crosby says about business in general is certainly true for software businesses. In this chapter, we'll introduce the major groupings of software patterns, or sub-cultures, and relate them to Crosby's work that he summarized in his "Quality Management Maturity Grid."

## 2.1 Applying Crosby's Ideas to Software

Readers who have read "Quality Is Free" will notice how consonant our views of software quality are to Crosby's views of quality in general. In particular, they will notice that we share the view that the critical factor is always "the people involved—their motivations and reactions." Even so, few people have had much success in directly applying Crosby's approach to software engineering. That's because, as we've said,

1. No two organizations are exactly alike.

2. No two organizations are entirely different.

We have changed Crosby's approach to account for the

differences, so we need to explain several areas in which our approach to software quality differs from Crosby's.

### 2.1.1 Conformance to requirements is not enough

Crosby is very clear in defining quality as "conformance to requirements."

"If a Cadillac conforms to all the requirements of a Cadillac, then it is a quality car. If a Pinto conforms to all the requirements of a Pinto, then it is a quality car."

That's an excellent definition as long as the requirements are correct. I'm not an expert in manufacturing, so I can't say how frequently manufacturing requirements are clear and correct. I am an expert in software engineering, however, and I can definitely assert that software requirements are seldom even close to being correct. If the customer wanted a Pinto and you built a car that conformed to all the requirements of a Cadillac, that is *not* a quality car.

Many writers on software quality have missed the point that software development is *not* a manufacturing operation. It does *contain* a manufacturing operation—the duplication of software once developed. Indeed, some of my clients have successfully applied Crosby's definitions and approach to making accurate copies of completed software. Software duplication, however is generally not one of the most difficult parts of software development (Figure 2-1).

| Designing/ Creating | Pseudo- Manufacturing* | Manufacturing |
|---|---|---|
| Requirements | Low-Level Design | Duplication of Disks |
| High-Level Design | Coding | Printing of Manuals |
| Documentation | Code Conversion | |

*Pseudo-Manufacturing operations have some properties of manufacturing mixed with some properties of designing and creating.

**Figure 2-1. Some of the processes in software development are manufacturing operations and some resemble manufacturing in a few of their aspects. These can definitely apply Crosby's approach to achieve high quality.**

In software development, therefore, we've had to generalize the definition of quality to the one we developed in the previous chapter:

*Quality is value to some person(s).*

Requirements are not an end in themselves, but a means to an end—the end of providing value to some person(s). If requirements correctly identify the important people and capture their true values, this definition reduces precisely to Crosby's conformance to requirements. In software work, however, we cannot assume this ideal situation, so much of the development process is concerned with more closely approaching the "true" requirements. Therefore,

33

much of what we need to understand about quality software management concerns this parallel development of requirements and software.

### *2.1.2 "Zero Defects" is not realistic in most projects*

Because software development is only partly a manufacturing process, Crosby's goal of "Zero Defects" is not realistic. It *is* realistic for the manufacturing *parts* of the process, such as code duplication and probably coding itself (once the design is accepted as a true representation of the true requirements). And perhaps, in ten or twenty years, it will be realistic for the design process itself, at least the low-level design (Figure 2-1).

However, in 35 years of software building and consulting, I've never seen anything approaching "Zero Defects" in requirements work. If you examine those software projects that claim to be "Zero Defects," you will find that they always start with an accepted requirements document, as in,

a. Conversion of a program from one language to another, where duplicating the behavior of the original program is taken as the absolute requirement. There are now companies that can consistently do such conversions on fixed schedules with fixed prices—and "Zero Defects" guaranteed.

b. Creating a program for a new environment, using a standard requirement , as in the creation of a new COBOL compiler.

Thus, for the foreseeable future, most of us will have to manage software development in a "dirty" environment, where requirements cannot be assumed correct. To ignore this reality would be to play the ostrich, not the quality software manager.

### 2.1.3 There is an "economics of quality"

Crosby says, "The third erroneous assumption is that there is an 'economics' of quality. ...The second (most often offered excuse managers offer for not doing anything) is that the economics of quality won't allow them to do anything. What they mean is that they can't afford to make it that good....If they want to make certain that they are using the least expensive process that will still do the job, they should get deep into process certification and product qualification."

Again, this assumes that there is a correct set of requirement to start the process. If the requirements are correct, then it is not the development manager's job to decide what is "gold plating" and what is essential. The requirements answer all such questions once and for all. If there is only one right way, there cannot be any question of the "economics of quality." As Crosby correctly says,

*"It is always cheaper to do things right the first time."*

However, when the customers' values are not known, and even worse when the customers are not known, then we don't know what the "things" are. We may produce things right, but

35

discover that they are not the right things. That's why the requirements process can produce or destroy value, and that's why there's an economics of quality, in any software project that includes a requirements process.

This "economics of requirements quality" certainly argues for getting the requirements right in the first place. If you can do it, then by all means take that approach. Where you cannot, however, the politics/emotions of negotiating value (quality) will permeate your project—and make it much harder.

### 2.1.4 Any pattern can be a success

In the examples of the previous chapter, we saw that even errors in conformance to formal requirements don't necessarily destroy the value of a software product, and that trying to meet every last requirement can result in destroying value for a subset of the customers. That's why the battle cry of so many software development managers is

Don't touch the program!

or even more conservative,

Don't touch the (software development) process!

Although this attitude is often ridiculed, it makes sense economically. If the way you now produce and maintain software is wholly satisfactory, don't work on changing it; work on maintaining it. If your customers are happy, it would be foolish to change.

As we'll see, collapse (of a program or a process) is an ever-present possibility for most software managers. If your customers are mildly unhappy, then you're probably in the right pattern, but not doing it as well as you could. Don't change your basic pattern, but improve it by small, safe changes that don't risk collapse.

But if you're currently in the *wrong* pattern, then trying to improve it by small changes is like creating ever more detailed maps for the wrong trip. If you're supposed to go from Miami to Cleveland, then detailed maps of the Los Angeles metropolitan area are not only useless, they are distracting. If your customers are unhappy, it will be fatal *not* to change. If you're not in the appropriate pattern, then choose the pattern that will give you the quality/cost you need and work within that pattern to do it well.

Quality is the ability to consistently get what people need. That means producing what people will value and not producing what people won't value. Don't use a sledge-hammer to crack a peanut. Don't use a nut-cracker to break up a wall. Choose the pattern that will give you the quality/cost you need and work within that pattern to do it consistently.

Working consistently is the essence of a pattern, or sub-culture. Working consistently to give value to your customers is the essence of success. Therefore, any subculture can be a success.

### 2.1.5 *"Maturity" is not the right word*

It's very tempting, when writing about cultures, to slip into a judgmental mode. For instance, it's hard for some people to believe that *any* software subculture can be a success. Like the pigs in Orwell's Animal Farm, they accept the words that say, "All animals are created equal," then add, "...but some are more equal than others." "Any software culture can be successful," they agree, "but some are more successful than others."

Most often, this judgment slips in covertly. Crosby, for example, describes five different patterns of quality management in his "Quality Management Maturity Grid." The Grid is a strikingly useful tool, but a better name would have been, simply, "Quality Management Grid." The word "maturity" is a judgment, not a fact, but an *interpretation* of facts. At the very least, it doesn't fit the facts. Maturing normally goes in one direction, but Crosby gives several examples of organizations "falling back, as in this quote:

"We were Enlightened (one of the "maturity" stages) for a couple of years, then we got a new general manager who thinks quality is expensive. We'll have to drop back a stage or two until he gets enlightened."

In everyday language, "mature" means "having attained the normal peak of natural growth and development." There's nothing particularly "natural" in the progression through Crosby's stages. Indeed, Crosby is at great pains to emphasize the vast amounts of work involved to change from one stage to another.

Moreover, I have observed many software organizations that have attained "the normal peak," in the sense that they are going to stay right where they are unless something abnormal happens. They are good enough, and investing in attaining another pattern would serve no organizational purpose. As we've seen, cultural patterns are not more or less mature, they are just more or less *fitting*. Of course, some people have an emotional *need* for "perfection", and they will impose this emotional need on everything they do. Their comparisons have nothing to do with the organization's problems, but with their own:

> *The quest for unjustified perfection is not mature, but infantile.*

Hitler was quite clear on which was the "master race." His "Aryan" race was supposed to represent the mature end product of all human history, and that allowed Hitler to justify atrocities on "less mature" cultures such as Gypsies, Catholics, Jews, Poles, Czechs, and anyone else who got in their way. Many would-be reformers of software engineering start their work by requiring their "targets" to confess to their previous inferiority. These "little Hitlers" have not been very successful.

Very few healthy people will make such a confession voluntarily, and even concentrations camps didn't cause many people to change their minds. This is not "just a matter of words." Words are essential to any change project, because they give us models of the world as it was, and as we hope it to be. So, if your goal is changing an organization, start by dropping the comparisons, such as implied in the loaded term "maturity."

## 2.2 Six Software Sub-Cultural Patterns

To my knowledge, Crosby was the first to have the idea of levels of process maturity. He noticed that the (mostly) manufacturing organizations with which he worked could be studied *according to the quality of their production*. If he knew the quality of their product, Crosby could make predictions about what practices, attitudes, and understanding he would find inside the organization.

Crosby's observation was something we organization consultants use all the time, an application of "Boulding's Backward Basis", which says,

Things are the way they are because they got that way.

In other words, you can study products to learn about the processes that produced them, in much the same way that archaeologists study levels of technology from the remains they dig up from ruins. Like the archaeologists, Crosby discovered that the various processes that make up a technology don't merely occur in random combinations, but in coherent patterns. Crosby named his five patterns:

1. Uncertainty

2. Awakening

3. Enlightenment

4. Wisdom

5. Certainty

based largely on the *management attitudes* to be found in each.

In their article, "A Programming Process Study," Radice, et al. adapted Crosby's "stratification by quality" scheme to software development. In his book, *Managing the Software Process* , Watts Humphrey picked up their work and identified five levels of "process maturity" through which a software development organization might grow. These patterns were called:

1. Initial

2. Repeatable

3. Defined

4. Managed

5. Optimized

These names were more related to the *types of processes* found in each pattern, rather than to the attitudes of management.

Other observers quickly noted the usefulness of Humphrey's maturity levels. Bill Curtis, of MCC, for example, noticed that a parallel classification could be made simply on the basis of *the way people were treated* within the organization. He proposed a "software human resource maturity model" with five levels.

1. Herded

2. Managed

3. Tailored

4. Institutionalized

5. Optimized

Our own work with organizations is guided by the anthropological model of "participant observation," so we tend to observe what's happening at the *bottom* levels, not just what management is doing and saying. We particularly look for *the degree of congruence between what is said and what is done* in different parts of the organization. Classifying organizations by their degree of congruence, we can match them to the other systems of patterns as follows,

0. **Oblivious**: "We don't even know that we're performing a process."

1. **Variable**: "We do whatever we feel like at the moment."

2. **Routine**: "We follow our routines (except when we panic)."

3. **Steering**: "We choose among our routines by the results they produce."

4. **Anticipating**: "We establish routines based on our past experience of them."

5. **Congruent**: "Everyone is involved in improving everything all the time."

This is the classification we'll use throughout this book to describe organizations.

## 2.3 Pattern 0: Oblivious

We have added this pattern to the five used by other authors. Although it is not a *professional* pattern, it is the most frequent source of new programs, and can be used as a baseline against which other patterns can be compared. In pattern 0, there is no software development organization separate from the software user. An example of pattern 0 would be my developing a special little database to keep track of my own pulse and blood pressure, a spreadsheet to keep track of my scores at Precision Cribbage, or a BASIC program to drive a simulation game in one of my seminars. I have no manager, no customer, no specified processes. Indeed, I probably have little or no awareness that I am doing something called "software development," like Moliere's gentleman who was unaware that he had been speaking prose all his life. If asked, I would probably say I was "solving a problem." That's why we call pattern 0, "oblivious."

Not only are the people using pattern 0 oblivious to their doing software development, but so are most writers on software development. I asked one of my clients, the Information Systems

Manager of a large corporation, to survey the number of groups working in each of the various patterns. Their estimates were:

0. Oblivious 25,000

1. Variable 300

2. Routine 2,600

3. Steering 250

4. Anticipating 0

5. Congruent 0

The Information Systems Manager told me he had never really thought about the 25,000 people in the organization who had been given access to PC's or time-sharing. He worried about what would happen when they became aware that they were doing software development. If they came to his organization for help, was that his job?

They would become aware, of course, only when their quality became unacceptable. What saves Information Systems Managers from the Oblivious is a psychological phenomenon known as "cognitive dissonance." How many people will admit that they don't value the product of their own hands and brain? Indeed, this might be called the pattern of the "super-individual."

If asked why they are using this pattern, the Pattern 0 people would probably say, "nobody else can give me what I want, or really understand me." The characteristic magic posture of this pattern is that of a god: Omniscient and Omnipotent. At times, playing god can be a lot of fun.

Whether because of fun, cognitive dissonance, or some other factors, Pattern 0 is highly successful at producing satisfied users. Based on our casual observations, it seems to contain a number of sub-patterns. In this work, we are not particularly interested in Pattern 0 except as a standard against which other patterns are often weighed.

## 2.4 Pattern 1: Variable

Pattern 1, Variable, often follows Pattern 0 when problem solvers become aware, rightly or wrongly, that they are out of their depth. It is the first of the patterns to involve a distinction between the developer and user of software, so it's hard for the developer to remain oblivious to the process of software development. Because this is the first pattern to have this separation of responsibility for quality, it's the first pattern in which *blaming* appears as a substantial software development activity.

### 2.4.1 The superprogrammer image

Crosby says of this pattern, "There is no comprehension of quality as a management tool," but we go a step further. A characteristic of Pattern 1 is that:

There is no comprehension of management as a development tool.

This pattern could well be called the pattern of the individual programmer. The ideal here is the "superprogrammer," and the slogan is, "If we succeed, it's because of a superprogrammer." A variant of this pattern has the slogan, "If we succeed, it's because of a super-team (led, of course, by a superprogrammer). This is the idealized pattern for Mill's "chief programmer"—a compact "surgical team" headed by superprogrammer. It is also the pattern described in hardware development by Tracy Kidder in *The Soul of a New Machine.*

### 2.4.2 When Pattern 1 is successful

Like all the patterns, this one is often successful. I commonly find this pattern in young companies producing software products for microcomputers. At the slightest provocation, any member of the organization will relate an elaborate "creation myth" about the heroic feats of the founding team. Often, as the new company grows, it evolves to Pattern 2, but retains the myths of Pattern 1. These myths have great value in recruiting new programmers. Thus, one of my clients spoke about the "small team" that worked on a project—later, I discovered that over 250 people took part at various times in its 3-year duration.

Another place where Pattern 1 is found to be successful is in a large organization where a "pool" of programmers serves some important group of specialists. Information centers are often

46

structured as programming pools, but often they are more specialized. In aircraft companies, I have seen the pool attached to the engineers; in an insurance company, to the actuaries; in a bank, to the foreign exchange specialists. These pools can be highly effective at satisfying the needs of the specialists, and add much value to the company.

### 2.4.3 The ideal development structure

The ideal development structure in Pattern 1 is "the star in the closet." If the project is patently too large for one star, then the ideal is the "skunkworks." A Pattern 1 organization may have some procedures, but they don't cover most parts of the actual process. Besides, they always abandon any procedures at the first sign of crisis.

In Pattern 1, Curtis says, the typical personnel practices might include:

• *Selection*: Find out if candidate saw yesterday's game.

• *Appraising Performance*: Hold quick review before leaving on trip.

• *Organization Development*: Build morale over a beer after work.

According to Curtis, "software personnel are treated as a purchasable commodity," but I think the word "commodity" is imprecise. Personnel are "purchasable," but more in the sense that professional athletes are purchasable. The commodity model is more often seen in Pattern 2.

In Pattern 1, purchasing a "star" is the only hope the organization has of improving quality. The belief system is very much like voodoo (send in a hair or the fingernail of the key player, leader, programmer.) or cannibalism (which gives you the power of the person whose brain you eat.)

Humphrey says that the first step in statistical control is to achieve rudimentary predictability of schedules and costs. Since performance in Pattern 1 depends almost totally on individual efforts, the variability in schedules and costs depends almost totally on the variability in individuals. Studies of individuals have consistently shown variations of 20:1 or more in schedule, cost, and error performance among professional programmers, so it makes sense that this is the level of variation we see in Pattern 1.

In Pattern 1, the best predictor of project schedule, cost, or quality is which programmer does the job, thus reinforcing the belief system characteristic of this pattern. The programmer gets all the credit, as well as all the blame.

## 2.5 Pattern 2: Routine (but Unstable)

Pattern 2 arises for several reasons. An organization may be dissatisfied with the tremendous variation in Pattern 1. They may never have experienced Pattern 1, but simply need to build software that obviously requires more than a small team. Or, the projects may not be that big, but do require coordination with other organizations. In any case, managers decide they can no longer afford to "leave the programmers alone."

### 2.5.1 The super-leader image

Crosby characterizes the managers in this pattern as "recognizing that quality management may be of value, but not willing to provide money or time to make it all happen." There are several reasons they don't provide the money or time

• They don't appreciate the value of what can be accomplished.

• They don't know what is needed to accomplish changes.

• They believe that pushing the programmers is all they need to do the job.

A programmer in one Pattern 2 organization said of his management, "They think they're managing a salami factory." This pronouncement characterizes both the management style and the view of programmers who would prefer to be working in Pattern 1. The prevailing myth in Pattern 2 is that of the super-leader: "if we succeed, it's because of a super-manager (but there aren't very many of those). If we fail, it's because our manager is a turkey." This attitude is expressed beautifully in the following excerpt from The Tao of Programming:

*Why are the programmers nonproductive?*

*Because their time is wasted in meetings.*
*Why are the programmers rebellious?*
*Because the management interferes too much.*
*Why are the programmers resigning one by one?*
*Because they are burnt out.*
*Having worked for poor management,*
*They no longer value their jobs.*

Managers in this pattern do institute procedures—because they've been told that procedures are important to keep programmers under control. For instance, Curtis observes that by Pattern 2, management practices might have changed to:

• *Selection*: Managers are trained in selection interviewing.

• *Appraising Performance*: Managers trained in appraisal techniques.

• *Organization Development*: OD plan created, morale surveyed.

Both managers and programmers generally follow most such procedures. More often than not, though, they follow them in name only, *because they do not understand the reasoning behind them.* That's why we call this pattern "Routine."

For instance, when Curtis observes that managers are be trained in appraisal techniques, that merely means there have been courses for managers. There is ordinarily no way to check on what processes managers actually use in their appraisals. When we do check, we find little correspondence between what the appraisal class outline said to do and what is actually done in appraisals.

### 2.4.2 When Pattern 1 is successful

Humphrey says that the Pattern 2 organization has achieved a stable process with a repeatable level of statistical control by initiating rigorous project management of commitments, costs, schedules, and changes. The operational word here, however, is "repeatable," not "repeated." A telling characteristic of the Pattern 2 organization is that they don't always do what they know how to do. Just when they seem to be doing well on a series of projects, along comes one "disaster" project that bypasses the procedures just when they are needed most. Worse than that, management starts taking action that further undermines the situation. Here's a memo issued by the manager of a project with a staff of 59:

We are now in the final push to bring Gateway to market. In the 10 weeks between now and turnover date, the following rules will be in effect:

1. Everyone will be on scheduled 10-hour days, 6 days a week. This is the minimum work week.

2. There will be no time off for any reason. All class attendance is cancelled. All vacation days are cancelled. Managers are not to grant sick leave days.

3. We must ship a quality product. It's everyone's

responsibility to reduce the bug count. Testing, especially, must become more efficient. By ship date, today's bug count in every area will be cut in half.

4. We must ship an on-time product. Further schedule slips will not be allowed, and all previous slips must be made up by turnover. Starting today, any schedule problems will be reported to me on a daily basis.

Any developer, tester, or manager who violates any of these rules will be accountable to me. Remember:

WITH TEAMWORK, WE CAN FULFILL OUR COMMITMENTS.

You'll be interested to know that this product was shipped on time, and the manager was rewarded for his stunning feat of management. Some people did disobey orders, however, and got sick. Moreover, the "bugs" were not cut in half. Instead, they more than doubled, and four months after shipment, the product was suddenly withdrawn from the field.

Such disasters are inevitable in Pattern 2 organizations. Later, we'll use detailed models to demonstrate why. The primary reason, of course, is that Pattern 2 managers don't understand *why* they do what their routine procedures tell them to do. Thus, when things start to go wrong, they start issuing counterproductive orders — such as ordering people not to be sick.

### 2.4.3 The ideal development structure

It's a characteristic of Pattern 2 organizations to be
desperately seeking a "silver bullet" to make a radical change in
their performance. For instance, they often introduce refined
measurements that make no sense in their unstable environment.
Or, they purchase sophisticated tools which are either misused or
lie on the shelf unused. This approach is what the anthropologists
call "name magic." To work name magic, you just say the name of
the thing: "structured programming," "CASE tool," "IBM"—and
you have its full power at your disposal.

The ideal development structure for Pattern 2 is a manager
supported by powerful tools and procedures. When the jobs are
routine, all the manager has to do is ensure that everyone does
every step in the right order. To do this requires "mana," the
personal charismatic power that resides in an individual. If we just
"put Jack in charge," everything will be all right. Unless it isn't.

## 2.6 Pattern 3: Steering

### 2.6.1 The competent manager

Pattern 3 managers never depend on magic, but on
*understanding*. Though there are many exceptions, the average
Pattern 3 manager is more skilled or experienced than the average
Pattern 2 manager. Pattern 2 managers often have come a
successful programming career with no particular talent for

managing, no training in management, no great desire to manage, no time to acquire experience the job of management, and no role models to show them how to manage. That may be why they so often overestimate the power of their position:

I took a friend of mine—an organization consultant unaccustomed to working with such programming managers—on a consulting visit to one of my clients. After three days helping me interview people to determine the state of the organization, I asked him what he thought of their management style.

"Evidently," he said, "the only style they know is 'Management By Telling.'"

Pattern 3 managers have a variety of skills required to steer an organization, so they don't have to fall back on telling when their project gets in trouble.

### 2.6.2 When Pattern 3 is successful

Pattern 3 managers either have more training and experience, more desire, or else they are stamped from a different mold. Their procedures are not always completely defined, but they are always *understood*. Perhaps because of this understanding, Pattern 3 managers generally follow the processes they have defined, even in a crisis. That's why they can successfully manage larger, riskier projects with a greater degree of success.

If you examine the "typical" project, Pattern 3 may not look spectacularly better than Patterns 1 and 2. In Pattern 3, however, more projects are "typical," because there are many fewer outright failures. When a project starts, you can bet it will finish successfully—with value to the customers delivered on time and within budget.

### 2.6.3 The ideal development structure

Of course, Pattern 3 processes are more flexible, because managers choose them on the basis of their most recent information about what is actually happening. That's why we call this the "Steering" pattern.

Life in a Pattern 3 organization is much less routine than in a Pattern 2 organization, and the programmers are generally much happier with their work. They often display contempt for Pattern 1 programmers who don't appreciate the joys of working in a well-managed operation.

Humphrey says that the Pattern 3 organization has defined the process as a basis for consistent implementation and better understanding. He adds the important observation that advanced technology can usefully be introduced into this Pattern, but no earlier. In Pattern 3, tools are actually used, and used rather well.

## 2.7 Pattern 4: Anticipating

Speaking at a recent symposium, Humphrey presented data gathered from DoD organizations and contractors who participated in assessment of their software processes. They found that 85% of the projects are at the lowest level of software maturity; 14% are at level 2; and 1% are at level 3. They found no projects yet at levels 4 or 5.

Our own experience is similar. I have seen projects, or parts of projects, that had elements that are said to belong in Humphrey's level 4, but certainly not an entire organization. Therefore, whatever I say about level 4 (or Pattern 4), is partial or based on indirect knowledge or theory.

According to Crosby, the Pattern 4 manager is similar to the Pattern 3 manager but sits at a higher level in the organization and has a higher level of understanding concerning quality management.

According to Humphrey's extrapolation of Crosby to software, Pattern 3 managers have procedures, which they understand and follow uniformly. Moreover, the organization has initiated comprehensive process measurements and analysis. This is when the most significant quality improvements in individual projects begin.

## 2.8 Pattern 5: Congruent

Crosby says that at stage 5, quality management moves to the highest level. Managers consider quality management an essential part of the company system, as in the American Express Company, where the CEO has named himself Chief Quality Officer as well.

Humphrey predicts that level 5 organizations will have understood and followed procedures, which everyone is involved in improving all the time. This provides the organization with a foundation for continuing improvement and optimization of their process.

## 2.9. Helpful Hints and Variations

• At times, it's easy to be misled about an organization's pattern. To take one example, Pattern 1 organizations rarely have much trouble with overruns, which might make you think they are at Pattern 3 organization. They reason they don't have overruns, however, is that overruns generally poor management, and in Pattern 1, there is essentially no management at all. Thus, there is nobody with the authority to make the "boomerang" actions that drive a project into overruns.

• When things are going well in Pattern 2, it's easy to mistake it for Pattern 3. Only in the reaction to adverse circumstances do the differences become clear. Both use planned procedures, but only Pattern 3 people know how to respond effectively to deviations from their plans.

## 2.10. Summary

1. Philip Crosby's "Quality is Free" ideas can be applied to software, though perhaps with several modifications.

2. In software, conformance to requirements is not enough to define quality, because requirements cannot be as certain as in a manufacturing operation.

3. Our experience with software tells us that "zero defects" is not realistic in most projects, because there is diminishing value for the last few defects. Moreover, there are requirements defects that tend to dominate once the other defects are diminished.

4. Contrary to Crosby's claim, there is an "economics of quality" for software. We are not searching for perfection, but for value, unless we have a psychological need for perfection not justified by value.

5. Any software cultural pattern can be a success, given the right customer.

6. "Maturity" is not the right word for sub-cultural patterns, because it implies superiority where none can be inferred.

7. We can identify at least six software sub-cultural patterns:
• Pattern 0: oblivious
• Pattern 1: variable
• Pattern 2: routine (but unstable)
• Pattern 3: steering
• Pattern 4: anticipating
• Pattern 5: congruent

8. Hardly any observations exist on Patterns 4 and 5, as almost all software organizations are found in other patterns.

9. In this book, we shall be concerned primarily with Patterns 1-3—how to hold onto a satisfactory pattern or move to a more satisfactory one.

## 2.11. Practice

1. "If the way you now produce and maintain software is wholly satisfactory, don't work on changing it; work on maintaining it. If your customers are happy, it would be foolish to change." For this maxim to make sense, however, you have to have a way of knowing "if the way you now produce and maintain software is wholly satisfactory." Describe how an organization can know this, consistently. Describe how *your* organization can do this, consistently.

2. If you can't keep your product stable, how do you know you'll be able to keep your process stable, and vice versa. (develop this)

3. The term "levels" has also been used for what Crosby calls "maturity stages." Discuss the pros and cons of the term "levels" for sub-cultural patterns.

4. Quality is value to the user, but managers and developers are also "users" of any software system. Discuss what happens when their standards are higher, or just different, from the "paying customer," so they are displeased to work on a project, even if it's "good enough" for the customer.

# Chapter 3. What Is Needed To Change Patterns?

*A group of programmers were presenting a report to the Emperor. "What was the greatest achievement of the year?" the Emperor asked.*

*The programmers spoke among themselves and then replied, "We fixed 50% more bugs this year than we fixed last year."*

*The emperor looked on them in confusion. It was clear that he did not know what a 'bug' was. After conferring in low undertones with his chief minister, he turned to the programmers, his face red with anger. "You are guilty of poor quality control. Next year there will be no 'bugs'!" he demanded.*

*And sure enough, when the programmers presented their report to the Emperor the next year, there was no mention of bugs.*

For Emperors who believe in name magic, it's easy enough to appear to change patterns. But if you want to make a real change in your software culture, you have only yourself to fool. Unfortunately, if you're caught up in a certain subculture, you're also caught up in its thought patterns—habits of thought which always tend to preserve the culture, not change it.

## 3.1 Changing Thought Patterns

As consultants, we've found that the quickest and surest way to classify organizations into similar patterns is by the way people think and communicate.

### 3.1.1 Thought and communication in various patterns

*Oblivious.* Individualism is the key. People just program, don't know they are programming, and will rabidly deny they are programming.

*Variable.* Emotion and mysticism drive everything. People don't use words in consistent way, and they don't seem to know how to count. Here's a typical quote from the repair log of a level 1 organization:

"This works under the most current sources... I've fixed several bugs and made a lot of changes in the application code since this release, so I believe that these fixed the bug."

Translated into precise language, this means

"I did a lot of big magic, so I drove the devil away."

To see these thought patterns in action, watch how problems are handled. Everything is reactive and individual, with half-cocked solutions based on poor problem definitions. There's lots of heat, but not much light.

*Routine.* Most reasoning is verbal, though some common and reasonably useful definitions are beginning to come into use. "Statistics" are used, but almost always misused and misunderstood. One manager explained that they couldn't start spending more time on requirements and design because, "We spend 65% of our time debugging."

In Pattern 2, there is an unjustifiable *certainty* about what is known. For instance, managers don't know who the 20:1 programmers are, but they think they know.

Another key thought pattern is linear reasoning—A caused B. This "single cause, single effect" logic works fairly well as long as things stay routine. Such oversimplified reasoning, however, frequently produces conclusions that are actually contrary to fact. Usually, this happens when something extraordinary arises, such as a project running late (which in this pattern, is actually not that extraordinary, but people erroneously believe it is).

Problem-solving is not much better than in Pattern 1. More people may be ordered to tackle major problems, so statistics may provide a better chance of reasonable solutions. Only short-term solutions are attempted, however, and these often have reverse long-term effects.

*Steering.* In this pattern, people use important words with precision. They can also reason graphically, and are not restricted to linear thinking. Because there is less blaming, they are less afraid to face problems directly. They usually consider side-effects of their solutions. Consequently, they handle emergencies better and are trying to become proactive to prevent emergencies.

Pattern 3 people may spend a lot of time debating about measurements, but they really have not yet gotten much benefit for their big investment in measurement effort. At times, their measurements are meaningless or backwards, and may get them into trouble. For one thing, their process may not yet be stable enough to make their measurements meaningful.

*Anticipating.* They now have stability of process, of measurement, and in their way of talking about things. Crisis may shake them, but it's no longer possible for a persuasive manager or customer to coax them, force them, or trick them out of doing things the "proper way."

They habitually think in terms of the future: "What effect will this action have." Therefore, what crises they do have are not caused by their own management practices.

*Congruent.* Presumably, this level of organization would talk and act with scientific precision. It would be hard to observe their problem-solving style because they will manage to prevent most problems before they happen.

### 3.1.2 Using models to change thinking patterns

I wrote this book to assist software managers in making transitions from one pattern to another, especially from Patterns 1 and 2 to Pattern 3. To make such transitions—or even to ensure that you can retain your present pattern—you must start with the quality of thinking. You can tell where your organization is by studying the quality of the thinking, and you can imagine where you want to go by imagining what thinking will be like, because,

When the thinking changes, the organization changes, and vice versa.

63

In this volume, we'll show how each sub-culture uses models —implicit or explicit—to guide thinking. At *all* levels, models support the need for clear, correct communication. Using explicit models is another way of talking to each other, supplementing the vehicle of words with a more pictorial, dynamic, possibly non-linear mode.

### *3.1.3 How precise should the models be?*

At some advanced stage of development—corresponding to Humphrey's maturity levels 4 and 5—managers will be able use such dynamic models to begin simulating their organization, so as to plan their future. These simulations can be used to predict project outcomes and play "what-if" games with different strategies—in order to optimize the development process. Originally, I planned that this book would be filled with such precise simulations, but as the book developed, I realized that Pattern 1 and 2 organizations lacked the stable base on which to build such simulations. Therefore, I decided to leave this subject to others and concentrate on the practical problems of moving to Pattern 3.

In anticipation of the day when large numbers of Pattern 4 and 5 organizations begin to emerge, researchers have begun to explore more precise simulations. For instance, the day after I handed the original manuscript of this book to my publisher, I met Tarek Abdel-Hamid at the Monterey Software Conference and discovered that he and I have been working on parallel but complementary paths for a number of years. He starts from the high end—how to model software projects to achieve Humphey's higher maturity levels.

I, on the other hand, start from the low end—how to get projects to be stable enough so that Tarek's more precise modeling can be even more useful. None of my clients has a sufficiently stable process, let alone sufficiently precise data, to make it possible to simulate for precise prediction and control. That's why the models in this book are simply exploring gross dynamic effects which you must understand in order to stabilize your development process.

### 3.1.4 What models do for us

In other words, there are many ways that models help you to communicate with one another in order to facilitate the move to a different pattern:

1. You need to discover differences in your thinking, early, before they show up in consequences in your projects.

2. By working on ideas together in a public medium, and by understanding the reasons for various project practices, you facilitate team-building, which you need on any successful project.

3. One your project gets going, very little of the vast amount of communication gets recorded, so newcomers have a

difficult time coming on board. A few sketches of project dynamics helps new arrivals get productive much faster.

4. Your diagrams of effects give you a record you can use to compare what you though would happen with what actually happened. This gives you a starting point for improving your models, and then improving your processes for the next time.

5. Although you keep improving your processes, controlling software projects will never become a routine job. You'll always require lots of creative solutions, and dynamic modeling gives you a powerful tool to help be creative.

## 3.2 Choosing A Better Pattern

The very first models we'll need to help us move to a new pattern are the general models of the patterns themselves. If you want to transform your organization from one pattern to another, you first must know what these two patterns *are*.

3.2.1 Is your present pattern good enough?

Once you understand which patterns you are thinking about, you must have a way of deciding which is better for you.

I took one client to visit another, to observe how they coped with software. "Oh, if we could only do that well," said the visitor, to which the host replied, "But this is terrible. Our mission is to scrap this way of doing things for something that's *really* good."

The descriptions of the patterns in the previous chapter were intended to help you decide where you are now. You next need to decide whether this pattern is "bad" or not. The following case study can help generate a model that will assist you in making that decision:

Case A. Purple Mountain Software has sold 10,000 copies of their Purple Problem Predictor (3P) at $400 each. They continue to sell more copies, but a major part of their present income is from selling new releases of 3P. On the other hand, a major part of their expenses is handling customer services (phone calls and visits to large customers) for these releases.

Their estimated cost of service per release is $10 per customer. A new release is being planned. They believe they could cut errors/problems to $8 per customer by spending another $50,000 to change the development pattern used for the release. Although they know how to change their pattern, they won't do it because it only saves them at most $20,000 ($2 x 10,000 customers who chose to upgrade).

In short, Purple Mountain knows a better way to develop their releases, but under these economic conditions, they won't use it.

### 3.2.2 Organizational demands

Pure economic logic is not the only determinant of development pattern. Management doesn't make decisions based on pure economics, but on their *model of economics*, as shown by

67

the following elaboration of Case A:

Another impediment to this pattern change is Purple Mountain's cost accounting. The expense of changing the pattern will occur in Development Manager's budget, but the savings will accrue to the Service Manager. To make such a cross-department change would require high-level management understanding and agreement, and nobody wants to disturb upper management.

Management's models of technology can also influence the choice of pattern in other ways. Consider the following case:

Case B. Suppose 3P knew of a technique that would change to this new pattern for only $10,000, instead of $50,000. Now, a $20,000 saving would look profitable, which shows how improving the technology of development changes the decision about what pattern to adopt.

Case B begins to explain why a pattern is a coherent set of attributes. At a given economic level, only techniques below a certain cost threshold will seem attractive. Organizations in similar economic circumstances will thus tend to arrive at the same pattern, but only if their information is adequate. Nobody will adopt a technique they don't know about.

### 3.2.3 Customer demands

What else might cause Purple Mountain to change their mind? Consider these slightly different cases:

Case C. Suppose Purple Mountain had 100,000 customers

who would buy the upgrade. At $2 saved per customer, the total savings of $200,000 would far exceed the estimated cost of $50,000. In this case, changing patterns would be worth the cost, though the cost accounting problem might still prevent the change.

Case D. Service calls are not a cost to Purple Mountain alone. If their customers perceive fewer service calls as higher quality, they may increase their purchases of 3P, or recommend it to their friends. Suppose this extra value of the release increases 3P sales by 1,000 copies. This increase in revenue of $400,000 (1,000 x $400 per copy) would also justify spending $50,000 to change the pattern in order to improve the release. But do they calculate these numbers? Or don't they see the connection between quality and sales?

Clearly, Purple Mountain's customers have a strong influence on the pattern they choose for 3D development, again assuming management is perceptive enough to understand their customers. If they're *not* perceptive enough, the realities of the organization will override the customer demands in influencing the development pattern they choose.

### 3.2.4 Problem demands

What else might cause Purple Mountain to change their mind? Consider these slightly different cases:

Case E. Suppose Purple Mountain has another product, the Easy Everlasting Eliminator. They estimate that they could sell

69

10,000 copies of 3E for $4,000 each. They would like to earn this $40,000,000 revenue, but unfortunately, 3E is a much more complex product than 3P. Using their present development pattern, they estimate development cost at $10,000,000, with only one chance in 4 that they would be successful at getting an acceptable product.

Clearly, if Purple Mountain wishes to get into the Eliminator market, they will either need to develop a larger market or adopt a new development pattern. To develop a larger market, they might have to add features to 3E, which could further increase their cost, or reduce their chances of successful development—unless they adopted a more effective pattern.

### 3.2.5 Choosing a point in "pattern space"

Figure 3-1 captures the essence of the lessons of these case studies. Given informed, effective management, an organization would choose its software cultural pattern based on two factors:

- the demands of the problems it's trying to solve
- the demands of its customers, or potential customers

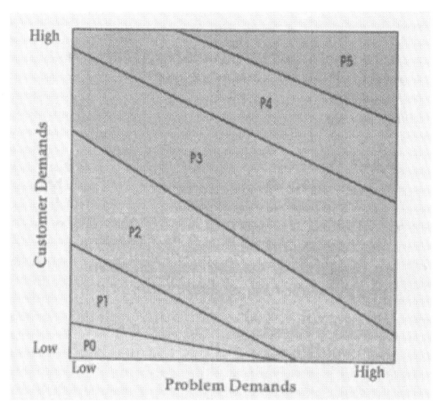

**Figure 3-1. An organization can be pressed to move to a different pattern by changing customer demands, changing problem demands, or both.**

An organization need not change in response to these demands. Sometimes, it can remain in the same pattern by trading customer demands for problem demands, in either direction.

Case F. Suppose Purple Mountain tries to extend the functionality of 3P, but finds that they cannot deliver these extensions without increasing the number of service calls. They can, in effect, make the customers less demanding by such actions as

    • lowering the price of 3P, thus widening the market

    • reducing the service level, as by charging for calls

Figure 3-2 shows the effect of such moves in the pattern space. If they succeed, these decisions allow Purple Mountain to leave their development pattern where it has traditionally been. Of course, if they have strong competitors, lowering prices may not widen their market, and customers may swiftly depart if the service level is lowered.

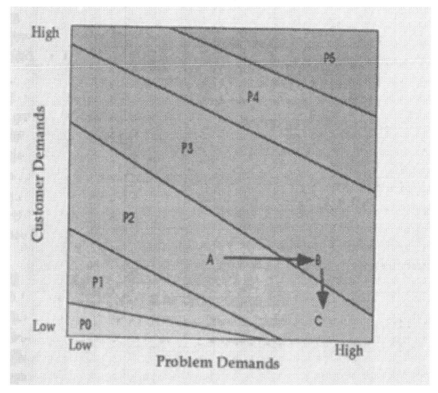

**Figure 3-2. An organization can retain its pattern in response**

**to increased problem demands (B) by reducing customer demands (C).**

Here's an example of a trade in the other direction.

Case G. Suppose Purple Mountain tries to extend the market for 3P, but finds that they cannot produce a version of 3P at a cost that will lead to an attractive price. They can, in effect, make the problem less demanding by such actions as

- contracting with a third party to develop the new version
- eliminating difficult functions from the requirements

Again, as shown in Figure 3-3, these decisions, if successful, allow Purple Mountain to leave their development pattern where it has traditionally been. Of course, their chosen third party may be no better at developing 3P than they are, and customers may not be forthcoming if functionality is less than a competitor knows how to provide.

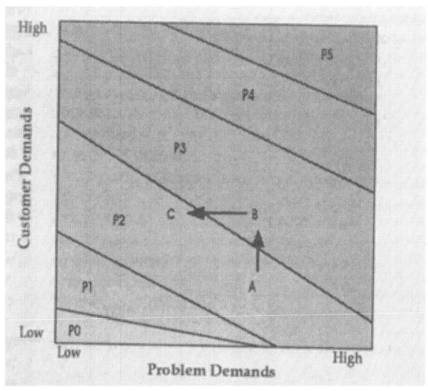

Figure 3-3. An organization can retain its pattern in response to increased customer demands (B) by reducing problem demands (C).

### 3.2.6 The temptation to stagnate

In the end, then, a development organization may be able to remain in its present pattern for a long time if:

- customers are not demanding
- problems aren't growing in difficulty
- there are no competitors to offer customers alternatives

For example,

Case H. Suppose Purple Mountain issues release 4.0 of 3P. It

74

fails so often that they issue a "fix release" four months later. A couple of features that were behind schedule for release 4.0 are added to make the fix release attractive. Development calls this new release 3P 4.01, and give it free to buyers of 3P 4.0. Marketing kills that idea and relabels it 3P 5.0, with a price tag of $45. Purple Mountain sells 10,000 copies, grossing $450,000 as a reward for doing a lousy job of development.

Clearly, Purple Mountain's customers are not very demanding and the problems aren't growing in difficulty, except for internally generated difficulties. Because 3P is the only product of its type, there are no competitors to offer customers alternatives, so where is the incentive for Purple Mountain to improve its software development. Indeed, there is a clear incentive for them to get worse, so the customers will be grateful for each new "fix release."

You may not approve morally of Purple Mountain's decision to become a less controlled software development organization. I certainly don't. But you'd better accept the fact that this sort of degeneration occurs all the time. Lacking outside demands, few software organizations can improve their development practices out of purely moral motivation. Quality may be free, in the long run, but in the short run, there will always be a cost barrier to making the transition.

Cloud City Software has a product with a dominant (90% market share). People buy this product because they recognize the name, and because they want compatibility with their colleagues who have already bought the product. In a meeting to discuss improvements to their software development process, the Vice-President of Marketing actually said, "We have the dominant product in the industry. Why would we want to change *anything*?" His argument carried the day.

Without clear business reasons to "jump the hump," Cloud City allowed its development practices to stagnate — even deteriorate. When a formidable competitor appeared on the scene, the Marketing Vice-President suddenly demanded development process improvements. Given this motivation, Cloud City invested a lot of their surplus cash in the effort, but in the two and one-half years it took them to shape up development, their competitor snatched away 47% of the market. In a competitive industry, short-term stagnation leads to long-term ruin.

## 3.3 Opening Patterns to Information

One of the reasons Cloud City couldn't revitalize its development process in a hurry was that a culture is a self-sustaining pattern that has remarkable powers of resistance to change. A great deal of that resistance derives from the thinking patterns themselves, which tend to be closed to ideas coming from outside the culture.

### 3.3.1 Circular argument

The principal device for closing a culture to information is the *circular argument*. For instance, consider these classics from our culture's past:

   • Women can't run a marathon without injuring themselves; therefore, don't allow women to run marathons for their own protection; therefore, never find out what women are capable of doing.

   • Blacks aren't capable of learning much; therefore, don't waste money on schools for blacks; therefore, never find out what Blacks are capable of learning.

Such closed circularities are repeated every day in the software business. They ensure that managers never find out what other patterns are capable of doing. Here's an example:

Some years ago, we helped a client make the transition from Pattern 2 to Pattern 3. The transition was necessary because they were producing telephone equipment that had to have down time of no more than one hour in 40 years! They were so successful in achieving their goal that their development manager published an account of the process. I was extremely pleased to have this written account because I hoped to use it as a guide for other organizations making a similar transition.

The very first time I showed the article to a Pattern 2 manager (in a beverage distributing company), he asserted, "That would never work here."

"Why not," I asked. "It should be quite straightforward. After all, their problems are *much* harder than yours."

"Their problems *couldn't* be as hard as ours."

"Why not? Why you don't even have on-line systems, let alone systems that have to respond in real time."

"Even so, their problems couldn't be as hard as ours because we could never get that kind of performance on *our* problems."

### 3.3.2 The classic software circle

And in case you think that his reaction was an exception, I should tell you that I tried using the article the same way three more times. Each time, I got the same reaction. Not being a complete fool, I stopped using the article and tried finding another way to break this classic software circle:

• We're doing the best possible job of software development; therefore, if other people seem to be doing better, their problems must be easier; therefore, we never find out what other people are capable of doing in software development.

Such circles close the organization to information from the outside, and are found in examples such as this:

• Consultants are carriers of bad software development practices; therefore, keep the consultants isolated from the other developers; therefore, we never find out what other consultants know about software development.

They also render the organization impervious to information from inside:

• Our superhero is infallible; therefore, if a project fails, it must be the fault of outsiders; therefore, we never look to discover ways in which our superhero might be fallible.

The outsiders are typically users, maintainers, operators, or consultants. The superhero varies from pattern to pattern. In level 0, it is the users themselves; in level 1, the programmers; in level 2, the managers. The

• Our superhero knows more about building software than anyone; therefore, if we have to investigate alternative ways of building software, assign the task to the superhero; therefore, we never discover ways to develop software that our superhero doesn't understand.

### 3.3.3 The key to opening closed circles

None of these false cultural images is easily refuted, except over a long period of time in which evidence accumulates in spite of the best efforts of the culture. The key question for opening these closed circles is this:

"Is your rate of success okay?"

Unfortunately, those patterns (0, 1, and 2) that need it most don't ordinarily keep records on their success rate. They also don't keep details on their failures and what they cost. As Barry Boehm observes,

"To date, there have been no studies establishing a well-defined productivity range for management quality. One reason for this is that poorly-managed projects rarely collect much data on their experiences."

The closure of cultures to information means that the first step in breaking a cultural pattern is to open it to information. In our consulting, we use a variety of tactics to start the information flowing:

• Establish a system of technical reviews so may people can see what's really happening inside their product.

• Send a few influential people to public seminars where they can hear about what other people do in face-to-face interaction, which is much harder to deny than ideas read in articles.

• Ask upper management the scientific question: "How would you spot a failure (or poor quality)?" Once we have their own definition, we take cases, one by one, and apply it.

### 3.3.4 Developing trust

Of course, to be able to do any of these things, you have to have established some level of trust, otherwise any sign of failure is used to measure and punish people. Patterns 0-2 are *power* hierarchies, each based on lack of trust:

0. We don't trust anyone but ourselves.

1. We don't trust managers.

2. We don't trust programmers.

Patterns 3-5, however, are *trust* hierarchies, which is why they are able to improve themselves. Higher numbered patterns do not represent increased maturity, but do represent movement from more closed to more open systems.

• Pattern 0 is only as open as the individual is open.

• Pattern 1 is open to exchange of information between developer and user.

• Pattern 2 is open information *from* the manager to developer and user.

• Pattern 3 is open in all directions to information about the *product*.

• Pattern 4 is open in all directions to information about the *process*.

• Pattern 5 is open in all directions to information about the *culture*.

Moving to more open levels depends on *creating the sub-systems that you can trust*. Why does trust work? The ability to trust sub-systems reduces the amount of communication needed to get the job done, because the amount of "checking up" is reduced.

Because trust reduces the need for data, increasing data flow is characteristic of a development system in trouble. Such a system lacks the information capacity to handle anything but the current crisis:

> • We're in deep trouble (because we don't know enough about building software); therefore, we don't have time to spend learning about how to develop software; therefore, we never learn how to stay out of deep trouble the next time.

If you have time to read this book, of course, you must not be caught in this, the most vicious cycle of all.

### 3.4. Helpful Hints and Variations

• Another great barrier to introducing change is *inertia from past success*. Inertia is like mass. The more success we carry over from the past, the more our past strength becomes our present weakness. For instance,

• Reusable code improves productivity, be may shut out improved solutions.

• Large volumes of code show that our services were valued, but may prove difficult to maintain.

• Past practices that have evolved through much experience may be so firmly anchored that nothing new has a chance to be given a fair trial.

• People's attitudes toward specific ideas may be influenced by past experiences in somewhat different environments.

• Regardless of what pattern we are trying to attain, there are three tasks we must accomplish. These tasks must be accomplished by any culture, as you can verify by studying the Bible or any religious guidebook to living.

• Present: Keep performing today; don't slip backwards.

( "Give us this day our daily bread.")

• Past: Maintain the foundation from yesterday; don't forget what you know.

("Honor thy father and thy mother.")

• Future: Build the next pattern, to guide the change process.

( "Where there is no vision, the people perish.")

Each of the six software sub-cultures works to maintain its past and present, but until you reach the higher patterns, this work is so difficult that the future gets left behind.

• What is necessary to move from one pattern to another depends also on which move you are making. Here's a snapshot of what specific learnings are required for each move, and where they might come from:

• 0 to 1: Humility, produced by exposure to what others are doing

• 1 to 2: Ability, produced by technical training and experience

• 2 to 3: Stability, produced by quality software

management

- 3 to 4: Agility, produced by tools and techniques

- 4 to 5: Adaptability, produced by human development

### 3.5. Summary

1. Each pattern has its characteristic way of thinking and communicating.

2. The first essential to changing a pattern is changing thought patterns that are characteristic of that pattern.

3. Thinking patterns consist of models, and new models can be used to change thinking patterns

4. In the less stable patterns, models need not be precise, but merely convincing. Indeed, precise models wouldn't make any sense without first establishing stability.

5. Models help us to:

- discover differences in thinking, before they have big consequences

- work on ideas together, to facilitate team-building

- understand the reasons for various project practices

- record communication so newcomers can get productive much faster

- maintain a record we can use to improve our processes for the next time

- be creative, because projects will never be routine.

6. Before you set about choosing a better pattern, you should always ask, "Is our present pattern good enough?"

7. The pattern you choose depends on a tradeoff among organizational demands, customer demands, and problem demands. These tradeoffs can be represented by choosing a point in "pattern space."

8. There is always a temptation for a software organization to stagnate by not choosing a new pattern, but instead reducing customer demands or problem demands.

9. The process of recognizing that a new pattern is needed is hindered by circular arguments that close the organization to the information it needs.

10. The key to opening closed circles is the question, "Is your rate of success okay?" Closed circles, however, tend to prevent this question from being asked.

11. Lack of trust tends to keep this key question from being answered truthfully, so organizational change often begins with actions for developing trust.

## 3.6. Practice

1. Recall an earlier question concerning the idea: "If the way you now produce and maintain software is wholly satisfactory, don't work on changing it; work on maintaining it. If your customers are happy, it would be foolish to change." Describe

cycles your organization uses that prevent it from knowing "if the way you now produce and maintain software is wholly satisfactory."

2. What are some ways your organization employs to reduce customer demands? What are some ways they reduce problem demands?

3. Vicious circles are not confined to information. A "lockon" occurs when a circular pattern of cause and effect reinforces the current state, which would otherwise be quite arbitrary. For instance, a country locks on to the "proper" driving side of the road. England locked onto the left side, while France locked onto the right side. If you drive on the right in England, the consequences quickly convince you to conform to the locked on local practice. In other words, when you try to change, forces are triggered that tend to counteract the change.

There are many, many examples of lockons that tend to hold a software organization in its present pattern. We will explore many of them in this book, after we develop some techniques for modeling and analyzing them. Before reading on, see if you can identify some lockons in your own organization's pattern, along with the forces that keep them in place.

# Part II Patterns Of Managing

Patterns of software culture don't just happen. They arise from the nature of software itself interacting with the nature of human beings. In particular, they arise from the struggles of human beings to control the software process.

In the following chapters, we'll see how each pattern arises from a particular human model of how processes are controlled. We'll learn how to describe those models and analyze them for their consequences, particularly for the instabilities to which they are subject. Then we'll expose several of the most common types of instability found in software organizations—how they work and what are their consequences. Finally, we'll study the types of control actions managers use in their attempts to reduce that instability, including those actions that succeed and those that actually make the situation worse.

# Chapter 4: Control Patterns for Management

*"Without deviation, progress is not possible."* - *Frank Zappa*

This is a self-help book. If you are not completely satisfied with the pattern you use to develop and maintain software, and if you can imagine that another pattern would be better, then this book is for you. In Figure 4-1, you might be at point A and want to solve more difficult problems (point B)—Perhaps you are implementing a network for the first time. Or you might be at point D and need to reduce the number of failures (point E)—perhaps your software is now going to be burned into ROM. Or you might be at point F and be faced with creeping increases in problem difficulty and customer demands (point G).

Or, if you *are* satisfied with your present position (S), this book can show you how to stay satisfied in the face of disasters just waiting to happen. In either case, you are concerned with control, and this chapter is about how each pattern has its characteristic pattern of control.

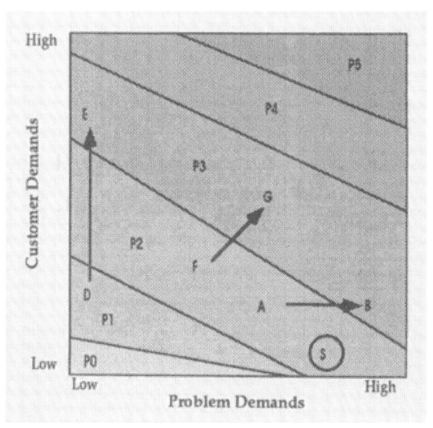

**Figure 4-1. This book is about moving from one pattern to another (A to B, D to E, F to G), or about ensuring that you remain where you are (S).**

## 4.1 Shooting at Moving Targets

According to Humphrey, most organizations today are found in Pattern 1 or Pattern 2. They are there because their problem demands and customer demands do not require them to be elsewhere. When one of these demands changes, however, these organizations begin to feel the pain. You can notice this happening because they tend to experience the classical grief cycle.

Their first response to control the pain is usually by controlling the information so they don't notice. When denial fails, they may suffer while blaming others, because people generally prefer familiarity to comfort or efficiency. When angry blaming fails, they try to remain where they are using by trading off one set of demands against another. If tradeoffs fail, however, they may reluctantly decide that they must accept a new pattern to retain control.

When do these demands change? The critical factor is how closely the success of software systems are tied to the success of the organization. An insurance company, for instance, may survive for decades with a Pattern 1 or 2 software organization—until one of its competitors manages to offer an on-line service to independent agents. A software company, on the other hand, may have to meet new customer demands almost daily, as competitors bombard the market with irresistible enhancements.

And, aside from these outside influences, there is always the slow but steady growth of customer sophistication. Just think of the word processor you bought five years ago, versus what you would buy today. To see this slow increase in demand, compare the way you developed software five years ago with the way you do it today. For one reason or another, software quality and productivity are *moving targets*.

When teaching someone to shoot at a moving target, you cannot give instructions about which direction to shoot, because the direction is constantly changing. Instead, you must give general instructions about aiming guns, instructions that can then be applied to a wide variety of moving targets. That's why the study of patterns of software control starts with the question, "What is needed to control *anything*?"

## 4.2 The Aggregate Control Model

One general approach to shooting at moving targets is the technique of *aggregation*. Aggregate control is like shooting with a shotgun, or more precisely, with shrapnel. If we simply send more bullets flying through the sky in sufficiently random directions, we will increase our chances of hitting a target, no matter how it is moving.

### 4.2.1 Aggregation in the software industry as a whole

The aggregate approach to software engineering would say, roughly: to be sure of getting a good product, start a large number of projects and choose the one that produces the best product. Indeed, if we look at the United States software industry, this would not be a bad description of some of our successes. For example, there are at present three Macintosh word processors that I think are reasonably good. But how many Macintosh word processor *projects* have been initiated in order to produce these three good *products*? I personally know of 14, and there are probably 140 that died before they got to my attention.

Is this a reasonable strategy? Perhaps not for the small, efficient Swiss, but from the point of view of the software *industry* in a large, rich country like the United States, aggregation is not as dumb a strategy as it first sounds.

### *4.2.2 Aggregation in a single organization*

From the point of an individual software company, aggregation may be a useful way to ensure success in special circumstances. For instance, companies building life-critical systems have developed two or three independent programs, each of whose output is compared with each of the others. This redundancy ensures a higher level of reliability than they could assure with one project alone, and is worth the extra cost.

Aggregation is most commonly found when purchasing software. Out of several products considered, you choose the best for your purposes. If your selection procedure is at all sensible, you should wind up with a better product than if you only considered one. Software salespeople, of course, are working hard to see that your selection procedure is not sensible.

Sometimes the use of aggregation is not fully intentional. Pattern 2 organizations frequently employ unintentional *serial* aggregation. When the first attempt to build a system doesn't turn out well, a second project is started. If the second doesn't turn out well, either, the organization may actually return to the first, now accepting its poor quality as the best of a bad lot. And sometimes the unintentional aggregation is *parallel*:

One of my clients started three linkage editor projects in an attempt to get one editor that was fast (X), one that was compact (Y), and one that was full-featured (Z). As it turned out, editor Y was faster, more compact, and had all the features of X and Z, so it was kept and the others were discarded.

In general, however, this type of direct aggregation is probably too costly for all software work. A Pattern 1 organization may get a better sales analysis report by assigning the task to 10 independent programmers and choosing the best program, but it's unlikely that we could sell that technique to company management.

### 4.2.3 Natural selection in a Pattern 1 Organization

Pattern 1 organizations do make great use of redundancy, but not in this obvious way. For example, one of the ways a Pattern 1 organization improves its productivity is through the diffusion of useful software tools. In this pattern, we don't find an effective centralized tool development group, nor do we find an integrated effort at tool evaluation or distribution. Tools simply diffuse from one programmer or team to another more or less by accidental personal interaction

In an aircraft engine company, a pool of 61 programmers

supported the engineers, one-on-one. We surveyed the use of tools and found, for example, that each of these programmers had at least one special job control procedure for running test traces of FORTRAN programs. In all, there were 27 different trace procedures. The most popular procedure was used by 12 programmers.

Our survey probably biased the diffusion process. One of the programmers decided to redo the survey 14 months later and found that the number of procedures was down to 17. 12 old procedures had disappeared from use, to be replaced by others. 2 new variants of old procedures had appeared. The most popular procedure (now different from the former leader) had 22 users.

This Pattern 1 use of the aggregate strategy is exactly analogous to natural selection, the process whereby variant species arise and are tested in the give and take of the natural environment. Natural selection guarantees improved fitness for any environment, but it is *very* expensive and slow. But, then, Pattern 1 organizations are often rich and laid back.

### 4.2.4 Why aggregation is popular in Pattern 2 organizations

Pattern 2 organizations are also heavy users of aggregation. Paradoxically, aggressive Pattern 2 managers often destroy some of the "natural" aggregate strategies with their enthusiastic, but ill-informed, interventions to "improve efficiency."

The Information Systems Department manufacturer of

94

packaging materials represents a typical Pattern 2 organization. In discussions with the management, we found the following examples of aggregation as a management strategy:

The management was vaguely aware of the "natural selection" of tools, as in a Pattern 1 organization. They seemed a bit embarrassed to admit that this "uncontrolled" activity took place, and assured us that they planned to create a centralized tool group—"as soon as the current crisis was over."

When one project was not ready on time (that is, at its fourth rescheduled date), they determined "which component was to blame," and assigned two of their "best programmers" to bring this component "back into line."

When one programmer quit "without warning" to return to college, they assigned another. They saw nothing unusual about this, because "programmers are always unpredictable." When we interviewed the newly matriculated student, she told us she had been accepted at the college in May. She left her job in September.

One current project was to build software to analyze telephone patterns and billing on their centralized phone system. This project was over two years late when a salesman from a software company visited. A week later, the salesman returned and walked out with an order for a telephone analysis package. The in-house project was killed and the people reassigned. Nobody complained.

As these examples show, aggregation is a frequent strategy in Pattern 2. Aggregation puts little burden on management, because it's is a way to get satisfactory products without knowing much about what you're doing.

### 4.2.5 Aggregation in other patterns

Aggregation is a universal strategy, and no pattern is without its examples. As we move to Pattern 3, however, we begin to see a more conscious use of aggregation and explicit manipulation of aggregation to aid in quality improvement. For instance,

A medium-sized, full-service bank created a product evaluation group that purchased multiple candidates for various PC software functions. They subjected them to comprehensive field trials, then chose the one or two top candidates to be required or recommended.

A telemarketing company was having costly problems with intermittent and unpredictable system failures with its network. When rigorous analysis failed to reveal the source of the problem, they offered a reward for any programmer or operator who could catch an example while it was happening and manually institute a trapping procedure. In a few days, they captured over 20 documented examples, from which their analysts were able to isolate the problem to one hardware component. When the vendor replaced that component, the problem disappeared, though they never did understand why.

This last example was pure hacking, but harnessed by wise management for maximum effectiveness. Hacking is the ultimate aggregate strategy, and there's no way to do without it from time to time. It appears in all patterns (with different frequencies), though some patterns seem to view its use with shame. Somehow, they have a feeling that they could do better by improving their aim *before* they pull the trigger—and, in general, we'd have to agree.

## 4.3 Patterns and Their Cybernetic Control Models

Whereas aggregation is like shooting with a shotgun, *feedback control* is like shooting with a rifle. Although feedback control has existed for centuries as a practical engineering model, cybernetics first studied feedback control explicitly in order to improve the firing of guns at moving targets, in World War II. Cybernetics, the "science of aiming," is a science that every software engineer needs to understand.

### 4.3.1 The system to be controlled (the focus of Patterns 0 and 1)

The cybernetic model starts with the idea of a system to be controlled (Figure 4-2). A system has inputs and outputs. For a system that produces software, the outputs are the software, plus "other outputs," which might include all sorts of things that are not the direct goal of the system, such as,

• greater competence with a programming language

• software tools developed while doing the intended software

• stronger, or weaker, development teams

• stress, pregnancies, influenza, happiness

• anger toward management

• respect for management

• thousands of failure reports

• personnel appraisals

The inputs are of three principal types (the 3 R's):

• requirements

• resources

• randomness

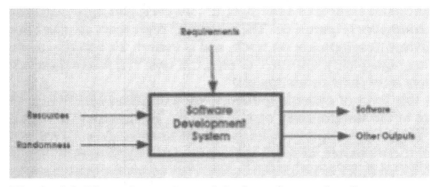

**Figure 4-2. The cybernetic model of a software development system to be controlled, which is also the Pattern 1 model of the entire process of software development.**

A system's behavior is governed by the formula:

*Behavior depends on both state and input.*

Thus, control depends not only on what we put in (requirements and resources) and what gets in some other way (randomness), but also on what's going on internally (the state).

Figure 4-2 represents the entire model of software development as understood by Pattern 1 organizations. In effect, it says, "Tell us what you want, give us some resources, and don't bother us." A bit more precisely, it says,

a. "Tell us what you want (and don't change your mind)."

b. "Give us some resources (and keep giving whenever we ask)."

c. "Don't bother us (that is, eliminate all randomness)."

These are the "abc's" of Pattern 1 software development, and by listening for these statements, you can reliably identify a Pattern 1 organization.

If you drop off the "a" (the external requirements) you get the identifying phrases for Pattern 0, which already knows what it wants, without help, thank you. Figure 4-2 can thus be transformed to the Pattern 0 diagram by dropping off the requirements arrow, thus isolating the system from direct external control. Of course, random inputs, or cutting off of resources, can disturb those individuals who are their own "software development systems."

### 4.3.2 The controller (the focus of Pattern 2)

99

To get more quality (value) from our software development with this Pattern 1 model, we would have to use the aggregate approach—in effect pumping more resources into the development system. One way to do this would be to initiate several such development systems and let each do whatever it does best. If we want more control of *each* system, however, we must connect it to some sort *controller* (Figure 4-3). The controller represents all our efforts to keep the software development on track, and is Pattern 2's addition to the problem of getting quality software. In effect, it says,

"I'll *make* those #$!@$&*# programmers meet their commitments!"

At this level of cybernetic theory, the controller cannot access the internal state of the development system directly. For instance, it's not considered kosher for the development manager to do brain surgery on the programmers to make them smarter, or to hit them with a blackjack to make them more motivated. So, in order to be able to control, the controller must be able to change the internal state indirectly through the inputs (the lines coming out of the controller and into the system). Examples of such change to the programming staff might include:

• offering training courses to make them smarter

• buying them tools to make them smarter

• hiring Harvard graduates to make them smarter (on the

average)

    • offering cash incentives to make them more motivated

    • offering more interesting assignments to make them more
motivated

    • firing Berkeley graduates to make them more motivated
(on the average)

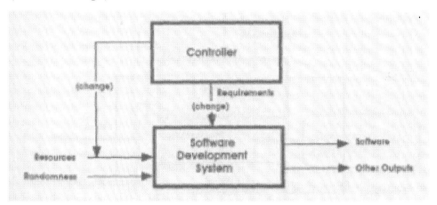

**Figure 4-3. A model of a software development system
controller.**

    The control actions are added to the system's *uncontrolled*
inputs (the randomness), either by changing requirements or
changing resources. Notice that no matter what the controller does
to these inputs, there is still "randomness" coming in, which simply
represents all those external things that the controller cannot totally
control. An example of randomness would be everyone on the
project coming down with the flu. Although the controller has
some control over the input of flu virus (such as paying for flu
shots), it is inconceivable that we would ever be able to guarantee

that no productive time will be lost to viral infections—regardless of memos to the contrary. This thought is most frustrating to some Pattern 2 managers.

### 4.3.3 Feedback control (the focus of Pattern 3)

An effective method of limiting losses due to flu would be to send people home at the first sign of symptoms. The Pattern 2 controller pictured in Figure 4-3 cannot do this because it has no knowledge of what the system is actually doing. A more versatile and effective model of control is the *feedback model* shown in Figure 4-4. In this model–which represents the Pattern 3 concept of control–the controller can make measurements of performance (the line coming out of the system and into the controller) and use them as an aid in determining its next control actions.

But feedback measurements and control actions are not enough for effective control. We know that *behavior **depends** on both state and input*. In order for the control actions to be effective, the Pattern 3 controller must possess *models* to *connect* the state and input with the behavior—models of what "depends" means for this system.

Overall, for feedback control to operate, the system of control must have

- an image of a <u>desired</u> state (state D)
- the ability to observe the <u>actual</u> state, (A)

- the ability to compare state A and state D for differences
- the ability to act on the system to bring A closer to D.

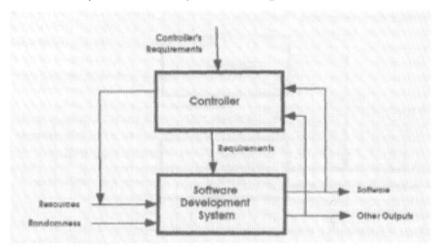

**Figure 4-4. The feedback model of a software development system requires feedback of information about the system's performance, plus requirements for the controller to compare with that information. This is the model that distinguishes Pattern 3 from Patterns 0, 1, and 2. It is also used by Patterns 4 and 5.**

### 4.4 Engineering Management

A characteristic Pattern 2 mistake is to equate "controller" with "manager." A dangerous tendency of Pattern 2 managers is to think, "If I'm not actively issuing orders, things are not in control. That's why they're always exhibiting *The First Law of Bad Management*:

*When something isn't working, do more of it.*

Managers certainly are controllers, but they are not the *only* controllers. In any real development project, there are controllers at every level, and everyone is acting as a controller some of the time over some of the work. To the extent that "non-managers"—or "small-m managers"—are controlling their work, the Managers' jobs are easier. They can *trust* the work to get done, so they have less need to communicate. And, when managers don't manage their work at all, the Managers can no longer trust the process—which makes their jobs become impossible.

### 4.4.1 The job of management

In the Pattern 3 model, managing is essentially a controller job. To manage an engineering project by feedback control, the manager needs to

- plan what should happen
- observe what significant things are really happening
- compare the observed with the planned
- take actions needed to bring actual closer to planned

(Figure 4-5).

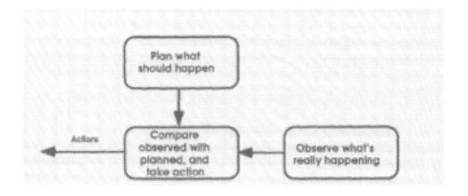

**Figure 4-5. In Pattern 3, management's job is to control a process that produces a desired product. Management plans what should happen, then observes what actually happens. Management's actions are designed on the basis of the difference between planned and actual results, then are fed back into the process being controlled.**

A big part of the manager's job is ensuring that each of these parts is present, because if any is missing, then our project doesn't have feedback control. Let's look at a common example of each one being absent from a Pattern 2 software project, when the project's managers thought they were in control.

### 4.4.2. No plan for what should happen

The first phase of project ALERT was scheduled to be delivered to beta-test sites on May 15, so when May 15 arrived, the project manager ordered the existing development version shipped. When one of the team leaders objected that several key functions had not yet been implemented, the project manager replied, "Look,

105

as long as we've not written down any requirements, they'll never know the difference."

This is a regression under pressure to Pattern 0 thinking — "We are the true customer, because we are omniscient." Although it's true that if there's no requirements document, anything you build matches the requirements *document*, it's not true that anything you build meets the customers' requirements. There is a world of difference between requirements and a requirements *document*. In this case, it happens, the customers *did* notice.

### 4.4.3. Failure to observe what significant things are really happening

Project EST used sophisticated project management software to "track" every software component in the project. For a component to be marked "complete" in the database, it had to pass a review. So, every time a team said their code was complete, the management held a "review."

Here were some typical comments from one of those "reviews":

- "The team has put in 235 hours, compared with the scheduled 180 hours."
- "Four weeks of elapsed time have been spent, versus 3.5 weeks scheduled."

- "There are 437 lines of executable code."
- "There are 63 lines of non-executable code."

Notice that none of these are observations about the *quality* (the value) of the work, but only its *quantity*—which is not surprising, as none of the managers had taken the time to inspect what the code actually did, nor were they qualified to do so. To their credit, the managers did interview the team leader, who was qualified to understand the code. She replied, "Yes, I think it's a good job. I know the programmers worked very hard on it."

This case is typical of a Pattern 2 organization trying to become Pattern 3. They've learned that the Pattern 3 manager depends heavily on observations of the true state of the project before taking actions, but they do not yet have a feeling for what makes an observation useful. Thus, though this review considered many "observations," none of them had much to do with the *quality* of what they're trying to control.

For instance, if the managers are trying to control "total time spent," the 235 hours spent on the component *is* a significant observation. On the other hand, it tells little, if anything, about whether the work was completed or not.

It's easy to see, though, how the managers could make such a mistake. If 180 hours were scheduled and only *10* hours were worked, that might indicate that the work was not completed. But it might also indicate that the programmer had created a very clever design, for we know that 18:1 variations in programming time for the same component are not at all unusual.

On the other hand, a *large* amount of time spent compared with an estimate may indicate that the work is completed, but in fact is more likely to indicate that the programmers experienced some unexpected difficulty—which, if anything, might make us suspect that the component was not finished correctly.

Or, if the managers were attempting to control project morale, then the team leader's remark about how hard the programmers worked might be a significant observation. Under the circumstances, however, it simply contributes to the false impression that this all too typical "review" meeting had something to do with controlling software quality–a typical mistake in struggling to convert from Pattern 2 to Pattern 3.

### 4.4.4. Failure to compare the observed with the planned

When project GATSBY—a comprehensive accounting package—was scheduled for delivery, the system test group announced to the management that the system had successfully completed a "volume test" of 37,452 test cases, most of which had been generated by a test data generator. Unfortunately, the managers failed to ask the system testers how many of the 37,452 test outputs matched the planned outputs. Management was so impressed with the sheer volume of this effort that they not only ordered the system delivered, but told their marketing department to put the number "37,452" in their advertisements.

Pattern 3 managers would have been suspicious of the large number of test cases, because, for instance, at even one minute per test, it would take over 15 weeks of full time effort to examine 37,452 outputs. Pattern 3 managers know that control is not possible unless actual output is *compared* with planned output.

After the system had been angrily rejected by its first customers, I was called in to "help with the quality problem." I discovered that the outputs were "sampled." A total of 136 "samples" had been carefully inspected. Of these, 43 were found to contain errors and were sent back to the programmers for fixing. After fixing, 19 were still wrong, so were sent back for another attempt. This time, only 6 were still wrong, so the system testing was declared finished.

When I asked why they had run the other 37,316 tests, the test leader told me, "We wanted to see how the system held up under volume testing. It was really solid. We were able to run the entire test without a single system crash." Further questioning revealed that most of the 136 "samples" had been cases that originally crashed the system.

You can draw your own conclusion about how many of the other cases were correct. We'll never know unless the bankruptcy court releases the company's papers to the public.

### 4.4.5. *Not taking action to bring actual closer to planned*

Project MNQ was already running late when component C37 —the system error handler—was put through a code review. The proper functioning of C37 was essential to every other function in MNQ, but the review revealed that its code was full of serious errors. Moreover, its design was clumsy and error-prone. The review's conclusion was that C37 should be scrapped, redesigned, and recoded.

The project manager, however, said, "We've got 6 months invested in C37, and we cannot afford a 6-month delay at this late date." As a result, the faulty C37 was used, which consistently caused trouble with the testing of every other component in the system. 10 months later, after the project manager had been fired, the new project manager scrapped C37 and set a crew to build a new one. They finished in less than 2 months, and there were essentially no more problems with error-handling.

The first project manager thought the project was under feedback control because they were conducting technical reviews. But if the manager is not willing to take an action that will result in a 6-month delay, what's the point of reviewing a piece of work that will take 6 months to rebuild? Without the possibility of controller action as a result of information from the code review, the review is a sham—a pseudo-review. If the project manager had no intention of acting when the information said to act, then the project would have been better off saving the time spent in doing the pseudo-review.

When top management has decreed that an organization will move from Pattern 2 to Pattern 3, the middle managers often conform in appearance only. Typically, they gather information, then don't use it. Upper management (who are also stuck in Pattern 2 mentality) often label this behavior "malicious compliance." Usually, though, the middle managers simply don't understand, having been given no training in Pattern 3 thinking.

## 4.5. From Computer Science to Software Engineering

What would it take for you to do a better job than these failed Pattern 2 software managers? Of course, you have to have many personal qualifications, but before we get into those, let's simply look at the inputs you'll need. No matter how clever you may be, the feedback model says you can't successfully control anything for very long without information. Figure 4-6 shows what information has to be added to Figure 4-5 to make the manager's job possible:

- What kind of product is wanted?
- By what processes can such a product be made?
- What's *actually* being made, by what process?

But to answer the third question without speculating, we must

111

have two conditions:

• We must have *visible* evidence on how the process is going on.

• The process must be *stable* enough so that the evidence is meaningful.

These conditions are generally *not* met in Pattern 2 organizations, which is why they remain Pattern 2 organizations.

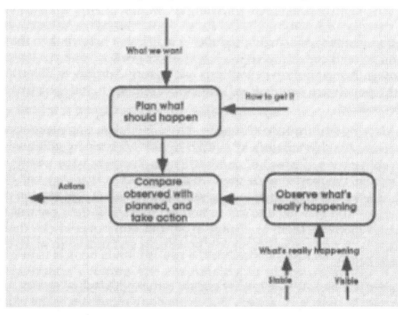

**Figure 4-6. In order to plan, management must know what is wanted and how to get it. In order to be observable, the product must be both stable and visible.**

Armed with these elements, you have the makings of a successful software engineer, consultant, or manager. All you have to do in out-of-control situations is look for which of them is missing. Hopefully, you'll be able to see that they're missing *before* harmful actions are taken. Unfortunately, the Pattern 2 managers in the four cases just cited were unable to do that, resulting in typical Pattern 2 failures.

I'm not sure, in each case, *why* the managers were unable to do the right thing. In order to control software, you do need to *understand* software development processes, and some of them certainly did not understand the simple fundamentals of feedback control. But understanding is not enough. Quality software development does not simply require a science, such as "computer science" or "cybernetics," but a *discipline*, an *engineering* discipline:

> *the application of scientific principles to practical ends*
> *as the design, construction, and operation*
> *of efficient and economical structures, equipment, and*
> systems.

If you want to be a software *engineer*, rather than simply a software theoretician, you have to master *yourself* well enough to be able to *apply* your understanding in taking action. As the Native Americans say, you must be able to "walk your talk." Although this volume will often emphasize the understanding, rather than the self-mastery, I'll remind you from time to time that it's always there, as the foundation for everything else.

## 4.6. Helpful Hints and Variations

• The essence of a pattern is what it can do consistently. It is possible to turn out single projects in a different pattern than the overall organization is capable of using—but not at a lower level. A pattern 3 organization never turns out pattern 2 products. If it tries to do so, the people are demoralized, the costs are higher, and the management is discredited.

• When trying to introduce change in software engineering practices (or any practices, for that matter), it's often better to work by addition, rather than subtraction. Instead of continually emphasizing what people are doing wrong, emphasize what they are doing right so that they will do more of it. Also, you can point out that there are things missing, but not too many at one time. You may need to say something about state B in order to motivate them to change at all, but don't overwhelm them with their sins. It only makes them feel powerless and unable to make any creative changes.

• Most writers on software quality equate errors with lack of quality, and lack of quality with lack of control. But errors don't mean you're out of control. You can set the level of errors that the customer can accept without loss of significant value, then control for that level. If you can't set and achieve your criteria, however, then you're out of control.

• Feedback control is often called "error control," because it is through the errors (deviations from requirements) that you get the information to control the system. Indeed, when there are no errors, the Pattern 3 control mechanisms remain dormant. (As Frank Zappa says, "Without deviation, progress is not possible.") In that case, an outside observer would have trouble distinguishing a Pattern 3 from a Pattern 2 organization. Moreover, the managers in Pattern 3 would have difficulty telling if they were in control or if their sources of error control information had dried up.

• Figure 4-5 is a key to feedback control. The "feeding back" of action is, of course, the origin of the term "feedback," but Pattern 2 thinkers are often befuddled when they first encounter this diagram. They think the "action" arrow points in the wrong direction. When the direction of this arrow becomes intuitive, they are on their way to becoming Pattern 3 managers.

• Although feedback control is generally much more elegant and efficient, remember that you always have aggregate control available if you're willing to pay the price. Last week a client of mine found a project dead in the water because somehow their configuration control system had destroyed the latest version of a critical routine. Everyone had to wait until the routine was found or reconstructed, so the project manager told all 9 people to each do whatever they could to find, recover, reconstruct, or otherwise get back the critical routine. Within 45 minutes, one of the programmers found an "erased" copy on an old disk. With the help

of a recovery utility, the project was back at full speed in another
15 minutes. Although it's true that the other 8 programmers
"wasted" an hour apiece trying some other method, they couldn't
have done anything useful with the time anyway. Besides, there
was no way to know in advance whose method was going to work
the fastest.

• It's not the purpose of this book to delve deeply into Patterns
4 and 5, but they are also intimately related to the Feedback
Control Model. Roughly, Pattern 4 management is applies
feedback control not just to the product, but to the process itself. In
other words, their "product" is the process. To make Figure 4-6 a
picture of Pattern 4 management, we should add an arrow from
"observe" to "plan."

• Pattern 5 management carries this feedback a step further,
while preserving what is good about Pattern 4. They apply
feedback control to the entire organization's culture—the
environment in which the Pattern 4 managers have to manage. In
short, in Pattern 5 we see a recursive nesting of feedback control,
at least to 3 levels of conscious management.

### 4.7. Summary

1. The Aggregate Control Model tells us that if we're willing
to spend enough on redundant solutions, we'll eventually get the
system we want. Sometimes this is the most practical way, or the

116

only way we can think of.

2. The Feedback Control Model tries for a more *efficient* way of getting what we want. A controller controls a system based on information about what the system is currently doing. Comparing this information with what is planned for the system, the controller takes actions designed to bring the system's behavior closer to plan.

3. The job of Engineering Management is to act as controller in engineering projects. Failures of engineering management can be understood in terms of the Feedback Control Model. Pattern 2 managers often lack this understanding, which often explains why they experience so many low quality, or failed, projects.

4. Projects can fail when there is no plan for what should happen.

5. Projects can fail when the controller fails to observe what significant things are really happening.

6. Projects can fail when the controller fails to compare the observed with the planned.

7. Projects can fail when the controller cannot or will not take action to bring actual closer to planned.

## 4.8. Practice

1. The aggregate approach is not always as expensive as it seems at first sight. For instance, developing three redundant

systems can improve reliability in life-critical applications, but doesn't it cost three times as much? In practice, the cost of triple redundancy is usually less than double the cost of a single system. Develop at least 3 reasons for this cost-saving effect.

2. A "good hack" is one that is done in full consciousness and opens possibilities for improvement. A "bad hack" is one that is done fuzzily and closes possibilities. Give an example from your experience of both a "good hack" and a "bad hack."

3. Give at least 5 examples of "other outputs" you have seen from a software development project. What information about the project did these "other outputs" carry?

4. Give at least 5 examples of ways a Pattern 2 manager might make the programming staff "smarter." Give at least 5 examples of ways to make them more motivated. Discuss what effects these ways might have on the "other outputs" of the development process.

5. Think of a project you know that did not perform satisfactorily. Analyze the management's control actions on that project from the point of view of the Feedback Control Model. Did the managers know about feedback control? Did they think they were using it? Were they, really?

6. Quality doesn't mean much if you can't *consistently* get what you need. One measure of a pattern is what size system it can complete successfully, say, 95% of the time. Plot a graph of this

measure for the different patterns. What level would be acceptable in your organization?

7. Suppose the managers in a Pattern 3 organization suspected that their feedback information about the development process were not reliable. Suggest what they might do. This is the kind of thinking that Pattern 4 managers must do, in advance.

8. Can the aggregate strategy be applied to the Pattern 4 task of controlling the process itself? Can it be applied to controlling the culture, as in Pattern 5? Explain your answers.

# Chapter 5 Making Explicit Management Models

*"More software projects have gone awry for lack of calendar time than for all other causes combined. Why is this cause of disaster so common?" - Frederick P. Brooks*

To keep software projects from going awry, the controller must have accurate and timely observations about what's currently happening. But that's not enough. The controller also must have an explicit understanding about the *meaning* of those observations. Has the system really gone awry? If so, why? Is it because of lack of calendar time, or something else? This understanding of meaning is what I call the controller's "system models." To a great extent, this volume is about the role system models play in software engineering.

## 5.1 Why Things Go Awry

In Figure 4-6, we saw that three kinds of information are needed to make the manager's job possible:

- What kind of product is wanted?

- By what processes can such a product be made?

- What's *actually* being made, by what process?

System models are critical to the second and third of these questions, because they affect both what you observe, and what you think about what you observe.

### 5.1.1 The role of system models

To understand the role of system models, consider an analogous control situation—keeping your automobile running reliably. When there's a click from the engine compartment of your car, the information is accurate and timely, but what does it mean? Here are three possibilities:

a. You don't even hear the click, because you are occupied with more important things.

b. The click sounds ominous to you, but the mechanic knows that it simply means that you need to tighten the bolt holding the washer fluid vessel.

c. The click sounds irrelevant to you, but the mechanic knows it means you're about to run out of oil and burn up the engine.

If you do hear the click, both you and the mechanic have the same information. Only the mechanic, however, understands how the engine works and thus can attach appropriate *meaning*. Without the meaning of the clicks, you don't know the right thing to do in response.

Any software engineering manager needs system models of the software engineering system for the same reason—to know what's important to observe, and what is the right response to new observations. If you overhear a programmer say that she found ten faults in one hour, is that important? If it's important, what does it mean? In this chapter, we'll begin our exploration of system models, models that tell us which software clicks are critical, and which can be ignored.

### 5.1.2. Implicit models

All managers use models to govern their management decisions, but in Pattern 1 and 2 organizations, most of those models are *implicit*. They may never enunciate these models, but by observing their behavior, you can see that they act "as if" the model were true. Here are some examples of common implicit models held by Pattern 1 and 2 managers and programmers:

- They will do what I tell them to do.
- They won't do what I don't tell them to do.
- All will go well.

- All will go well, unless I have bad luck.

- Most software projects go awry for lack of calendar time.

- If I'm behind schedule, I can add people to make things go faster.

- Bugs occur at random.

- If I tell them not to have bugs, then bugs will be reduced.

- The more pressure, the faster they'll work.

- The customer is trying to make me look bad.

- The customer is out to get something for nothing.

- The customer is a nice guy.

- The vice-president is my only customer.

- Managers don't understand programming.

- Managers do understand programming.

- Managers should understand programming.

- Managers shouldn't understand programming.

- Programmers don't understand management.

- Programmers understand management better than most managers.

- Twice as big a system will take twice as long, unless we use twice the people.

- Software development is a sequential process.

- If we find 10 faults in one day, we'll find 100 faults in 10 days.

- We'll never find all the faults, so we'll never be done.

- If I can measure it, I can control it.

- If I can't measure it, it's not important.

- Women make better programmers.

- Women are better at maintenance; men are better at design.

- Programmers lose their ability after age 30.

- Older programmers are more valuable.

- There's no difference in ability between men and women.

- The best programmers do the best job, and I know who they are.

- I know what's going on.

- If things go wrong, there's always somebody to blame.

- If things go right, it's because of good management.

- If things go wrong, it's an act of God.

You may agree or disagree with each of these models, but when they are not explicit, its difficult to discuss them. And, if they can't be discussed, they they can't be tested and improved. And, if the system models can't be improved, then you can't move to a different cultural pattern—or even be sure of staying in your present pattern. That's why, in this chapter, we'll introduce a notation for making system models explicit.

### 5.1.3 Inability to face reality

Many researchers, consultants, and observant software workers have studied the dynamics of software failure, and each has offered at least one explicit model of the process. Perhaps the most influential of these people has been Frederick P. Brooks. Brooks's *The Mythical Man-Month* was one of the first books to make explicit models of why software development is so troublesome. His vivid metaphor of the tar pit has stood the test of time, and Brooks's Law has become one of the Ten Commandments of software development. Because of this familiarity, Brooks's thinking provides compelling examples for exploring how models can be described and interpreted.

Over the years, I have learned much from Fred Brooks. I hope he will not feel I am presuming on our friendship if I take issue with one of his basic models, one which is contained in the quotation that heads this chapter. Although it certainly *seems* that way to the harried manager, lack of calendar time is not the *reason* software projects have gone awry. Instead, lack of calendar time is merely the reason other failures have been *detected*.

Because Pattern 1 and 2 organizations have lacked meaningful measurements and system models to interpret them, any meaningful measurement they do have take on exaggerated proportions. And one thing about calendar time: it has a meaning that most of us can understand. When the calendar says it's April

15, and the due date is April 15, and the software isn't done, even the dullest manager knows that we've missed our due date!

That's why I would rephrase Brooks's model by saying:

*Lack of calendar time has forced more failing software projects*

*to face the reality of their failure than all other reasons combined.*

And this could be rephrased as:

*Lack of calendar time has forced more failing software projects*

*to face the incorrectness of their models than all other reasons combined.*

### 5.1.4 Incorrect models

Brooks gives five failure dynamics to support why calendar time seems so important. Each of these failure dynamics is an important model of software engineering, and each failure is based on at least one faulty system model, as explained in parentheses below:

1. Estimating techniques are poorly developed, and based on the assumption that all will go well.

[Estimating, of course, depends on a model of the process being estimated. "All will go well" is a deep model, underlying many estimating models, especially the implicit ones.]

2. Estimating techniques confuse effort with progress.

[A common modeling mistake is not distinguish between two

variables which are closely correlated under some circumstances, but not under all circumstances, as are effort and progress. Sometimes more effort means less progress. Other examples of models expressing such a faulty correlation: lines of code written versus progress; orders issued versus effectiveness of management; machine capacity versus tool support.]

3. Software managers lack the personal effectiveness to be "courteously stubborn."

[This may indeed be a matter of personal effectiveness, but the inability to be courteously stubborn could also arise from a lack of models concerning what to be stubborn about. If you don't think it's important for programmers to be free from interruptions, you're not likely to be stubborn about a working environment that discourages random interruptions.]

4. Schedule progress is poorly monitored, partly because we have learned little from other engineering disciplines.

[Brooks implies—and I wholeheartedly agree—that software development is a type of engineering process, so that something could be learned from studying other engineering disciplines. More specifically, what could be learned is certain system models that are general enough to apply to any engineering development process.]

5. Managers tend to add "manpower" when they recognize a schedule slippage.

[The faulty model believes that more people make things go faster. Brooks offered a different model—the famous Brooks's Law—which I'll discuss below.]

In the years since the publication of *The Mythical Man-Month*, many software organizations have made progress on each of these dynamics of failure. But even when they've mastered *all* of them, they may still be stuck in the tar pit. Five dynamics doesn't begin to tell the story of software development

There are dozens of important software system models, each describing at least one dynamic, or combination of behaviors forced by the structure of the model. To take one example, Brooks's mixing of symptom and cause led him to miss a system dynamic that is much more frequently seen today. We could easily argue for this model:

*More software projects have gone awry for lack of quality,*
*which is part of many destructive dynamics,*
*than for all other causes combined.*

In other words, when quality starts to slip, so many dynamic forces are set in motion that most Pattern 1 and 2 managers are overwhelmed. Brooks's title, *The Mythical Man Month*, is taken from Brooks's Law, which describes how adding "man-months" late in a project "begins a regenerative cycle which ends in disaster." If we really want to know why "more software projects

127

have gone awry," Brooks's Law points toward the true villain:

*More software projects have gone awry from management taking action*

*based on incorrect system models than for all other causes combined.*

In other words, it's not any particular dynamic that causes the most problems, but misunderstanding the model behind the dynamic.

5.2 Linear Models and Their Fallacies

The big mistake made most by software managers is choosing a *linear* model when non-linear forces are at work. By all accounts, management everywhere seems to make this modeling mistake. One of the most common examples of such linear modeling is the assumption that the same pattern that produced quality small systems will also produce quality large systems.

Software life would certainly be comfortable if this linear model were true. Unfortunately, the difficulty of producing quality systems is exponentially related to system size and complexity, so as software gets bigger and more complex, old patterns quickly become inadequate. In many cases, the old patterns actually exacerbate the problems they are attempting to solve.

The assumption that "big is just the same as small, only bigger," is a model, a linear model. I've given this model a name, the "Scaling Fallacy," because it's important to remember as we explore software dynamics. It's important because

a. it's held by the great majority of Pattern 2 managers

b. it usually leads them into software crises.

### 5.2.1 Addititivity fallacies

To understand the importance of non-linear dynamics, we must start by understanding the difference between linear and non-linear models. Most of the time, if we don't consciously reflect upon the way we are thinking, we tend to use *linear* models. In a linear model, $1 + 1 = 2$, rather than 2 + some correction factor. If we get \$1 from Denise and \$1 from Sid, we have \$2. If we get a month's worth of code from Denise and a month's code from Sid, we have 2 months worth of code.

It's easy to see from the second example how linear models might not accurately reflect the reality of the situation. Denise and Sid may work independently, in which case the linear model would be workable. On the other hand, they might interact, in which case we may get some non-linearity. They may waste time communicating with one another, in which case,

$1 + 1 = 2$ - interference loss

They may stimulate one another to greater efforts, in which case,

$1 + 1 = 2$ + stimulation gain

Or, there may be both losses and gains, in which case,

$1 + 1 = 2$ + stimulation gain - interference loss

In the case of Brooks's Law, adding people to a task late in a project increased the amount of work to be done because of coordination problems, and decreased the available time of the experienced workers, because of training time for the new workers (Figure 5-1). Project managers got into trouble, Brooks said, by believing in the myth of the "man-month," which is a linear fallacy. It says that a month added to a month is two months, no matter whose month it is, and no matter when it is done.

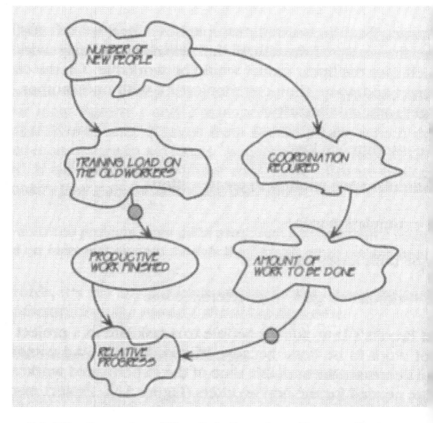

**Figure 5-1. The dynamics of Brooks's Law, in a diagram that shows why it is non-linear. The notation will be explained in Section 5.3.**

130

### 5.2.2 Scaling fallacies

Linear models are easy to use because they have the property of scaling up, so that if $1 + 1 = 2$, then $100 + 100 = 200$. If Arnette, their manager, plans for Denise and Sid to spend 100 days working together, she might get a big surprise when their one day's work doesn't scale up to 100 days. It might happen that when Denise and Sid work together for one day, the gains and losses happen to cancel out, so Arnette might easily conclude that their work is additive. She'll then be surprised to discover that although $1 + 1 = 2$, $100 + 100$ does not $= 200$.

For instance, the interference loss might be only a start-up effect, and not cost much once Denise and Sid know how to work together. Or, the interference loss might grow greater with time, if Denise and Sid learn to dislike each other and try to subvert each others' work. Managers who assumes that these effects won't occur expose themselves to committing the Scaling Fallacy:

*Large systems are like small systems, just bigger.*

One form of this fallacy applied to labor is Brooks's Law. Perhaps the most interesting question is why, now that the law has been so well documented, managers continue to ignore it and add people late in projects.

Managers (and others) commit scaling fallacies because linear models are often a useful first approximation for planning purposes. When presented with a new problem that seems twice as

131

big as the previous one, we make a "guesstimate" that it will require twice as much effort. This might be a satisfactory point for beginning our estimating process, but we'll get in trouble if we stop there. The real world is very seldom linear. That's why so many of our management illusions arise from assuming linearity when it doesn't apply. And that's why it's best to check for Scaling Fallacies and other common causes of non-linearity before taking any action based on our linear models.

### 5.3 The Diagram of Effects

One of the reasons we trap ourselves with linear models is that written and spoken language tend to be linear—in the sense of saying one thing at a time. Therefore, when we think or talk about a model in words, it can be very difficult to express non-linearities. That's why diagrams are often help us to grasp how things interact, and why systems thinkers have a tool kit of diagrams ready to use at a moment's notice.

One of the favorite systems descriptions tools is the diagram of effects . Figure 5-1, of Brooks's Law, for example, is a diagram of effects. A diagram of effects consists primarily of nodes connected by arrows:

1. Each node stands for a measurable quantity, like work produced, hours worked, errors created, or errors located. I use the "cloud" symbol rather than a circle or rectangle to remind us that

132

nodes indicate measurements, not things or processes as in flow charts, data flow diagrams, and the like.

2. These cloud nodes may represent actual measurements, or they may represent conceptual measurements—things that could be measured, but are not measured at present. They may be too expensive to measure, or not worth the trouble, or just not happen to be measured yet. The important thing is that they could be measured—perhaps only approximately—if we were willing to pay the price.

3. Sometimes, when I wish to indicate an actual measurement currently being made, I use a very regular, elliptical "cloud," as we see on the cloud labelled, "Productive work finished." Most of the time, however, we'll use effects diagrams for conceptual —rather than mathematical—analysis, so most of the clouds will be appropriately rough.

4. An arrow from node A to node B indicates that quantity A has an effect on quantity B. We may actually know the mathematical dynamic of the effect (such as,

Relative progress = Productive work finished / Amount of work to be done)

or it may be deduced from observations (as when we watch new people being trained by experienced people), or it may be inferred from past experience (as adding new people will increase the coordination required).

5. The general direction of the effect of A on B may be indicated by the presence or absence of the gray dot on the arrow between them.

a. No dot means that as A moves in one direction, B moves in the same direction. (More coordination means more work to be done; less coordination means less work to be done.)

b. A dot on the arrow means that as A moves in one direction, B moves in the opposite direction. (More work to be done means less relative progress; less work to be done means more relative progress.)

6. Later, we will introduce other conventions for the diagram of effects, but for now, we can do useful work with this small set of symbols to give a recognizable graphic representation.

### 5.4 Developing a Diagram of Effects from Output Backwards

Let's work through a simple example to see how the diagram of effects helps us to create system models that in turn help us reason about system dynamics. For the moment, to avoid controversy, let's confine ourselves to an example only remotely connected to software engineering. Suppose you are a programmer working on a project that is slipping behind schedule. You notice that you seem to be suffering from back problems that are often severe enough to prevent you from working. Obviously, the more frequent these back problems, the less will be your programming productivity. In order to help get your project back on schedule, you decide to study the dynamics of your back problems by creating a model.

### 5.4.1. Starting with the output

The most common way to develop a diagram of effects is to start with the quantity whose behavior most interests you. In this case, the quantity might be something like:

a. number of incidents of back pain

b. number of doctor visits with back pain

c. work time lost due to back problems

Each measure has certain advantages:

(a) is a direct measure easily obtained from studying your calendar

(b) may be a closer measure of severity of the back problems

(c) may be harder to measure, but is closer to our true interest—productivity

### 5.4.2. Brainstorming backwards effects

Suppose we choose (c). The next step is to brainstorm all the possible measures that might work through some mechanism to have an effect on "work time lost due to back problems." This might give us a list such as:

1. Your weight might increase your back problems because of

the greater leverage on your spine in all your activities, and the greater compression of disks between your vertebrae.

2. The amount you exercise might decrease your back problems because you strengthen your back muscles (as long as the exercise is appropriate for this purpose).

3. The kind of chair you use may affect your back problems, but "kind of chair" is not a measurable quantity. To use this effect, you would have to imagine a scale of something like "orthopedic quality of chair." If you can't think of how to measure it, even conceptually, you can't use it in the diagram. This doesn't mean you can experiment with different chairs to establish some sort measure of "orthopedic quality." Indeed, this kind of effort to establish metrics often yields the greatest benefits from the modeling effort.

### 5.4.3. Charting the backwards effects

Suppose these are all the effects we can think of, and that we decide to discard (3). In Figure 5-2, we see a simple diagram of effects showing how your weight and exercise might affect the amount of work lost. One arrow indicates that more weight increases the amount of work lost, while less weight decreases the work lost. The dot on the other arrow indicates that more exercise decreases the amount of work lost, and vice versa.

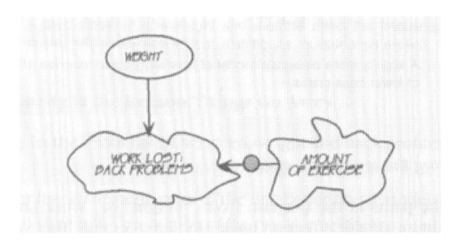

**Figure 5-2. A model of how weight and exercise affect the amount of work lost.**

This diagram of effects represents a very simple model. The point of the model, however, is not to be elaborate, or even correct, but to stimulate thinking. Those of us who have suffered from back problems can look at this diagram and begin a discussion of what it leaves out and what it distorts, based on our own experience. As the discussion continues, we can create new diagrams that hopefully reflect increasingly accurate and useful models. We will, in fact, elaborate upon this simple linear model as the chapter unfolds, showing how various non-linear models could be diagrammed.

### 5.4.4. Charting secondary effects

Increased weight seems to increase the work lost from back problems. The most obvious reason is that more weight puts more of a load on the back, but there might be less direct effects as well.

The next step is to brainstorm other connections among the nodes on the diagram. For example, more weight can lead to less exercise, because we feel more tired and less willing to get off the couch and go to the gym. Similarly, less weight could energize us to exercise more.

If we believe this effect might be significant, we add the arrow from Weight to Amount of Exercise, thus producing Figure 5-3, a slightly more elaborate model.

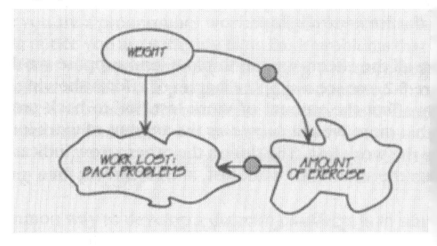

**Figure 5-3. A slightly more elaborate model of how weight and exercise affect the frequency of lower back crises.**

### 5.4.5. Tracing the secondary effects

By tracing the paths in the diagram from Weight to Work Lost, you see that weight has a double effect on back problems, because there are two different paths—one direct and one through Amount of Exercise—from Weight to Work Lost.

As you trace each indirect path, keep track of the dots along the path. Two dots (or any even number) along a path represent two inverse effects—and thus cancel each other. An additional increase in back problems is indirectly caused by increased weight decreasing exercise. Thus, the diagram suggest that a 10% increase in weight might lead to more than 10% increase in work lost.

5.4.6. Explicitly indicating multiplicative effects

This increase in work lost might still be linear, though disproportionate to the weight increase. A 10% increase in weight might produce a 20% increase in back pains, a 20% increase in weight might produce a 40% increase in back pains, and so forth.

On the other hand, we might have medical reasons to expect that the effects of exercise and weight are not simply additive. In that case, we might want to indicate the multiplicative effect explicitly. Figure 5-4 shows how we could indicate an interaction between the two effects of weight on back problems by connecting the effects arrows before they enter the Work Lost node. Usually, however, we don't need this convention, because we are seeking other non-linear effects that are even more powerful than simple multiplication.

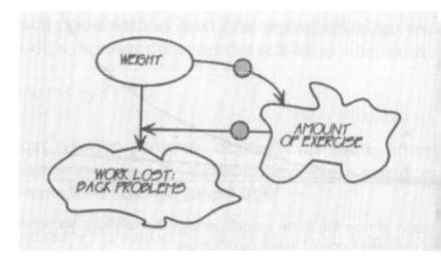

**Figure 5-4. A third model of how weight and exercise affect the frequency of lower back crises, with interaction effects, making the multiplication explicit.**

## 5.5. Non-linearity Is the Reason Things Go Awry

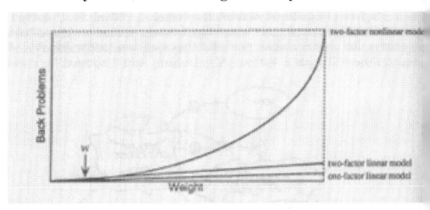

**Figure 5-5. A graph of how the three models predict the relationship between weight increases and the frequency of lower back crises.**

Figure 5-5 graphs the relationship between weight and work

140

lost for different models:

- The lower line is the prediction of the one-effect linear model of Figure 5-2.

- The middle line is the prediction of the 2-effect linear model in Figure 5-3.

- The curved line is the prediction of the multiplicative model in Figure 5-4.

For a small increases in weight, symbolized by point W, the three models are very similar. Moreover, these are very smooth model curves, omitting numerous real-world factors that add "noise" to any observations. Using observations from a 1% weight increase, it would be easy to fool yourself about which model was going to predict the future of your back pain. As your weight increased, however, the difference between the models becomes increasingly significant, even when masked by noise.

When you have a small weight gain, you can most easily do something to prevent back problems, but unfortunately that's the time you're least likely to be aware of impending difficulty. That's why you can't depend on observations alone to tell you that you may have a problem. By the time your observations tell you something's wrong, your back may have become exceedingly non-linear. They may be so big that the amount of exercise you'd need each day to be helpful out would prove dangerous to your back.

This situation is similar to Brooks's managers estimating project effort using a linear model. By the time they become aware that their estimates have gone astray, they've gone so far astray that it's difficult to bring the project back on course. Indeed, the size of the intervention needed to close the gap may be so big that it's likely to cause more disturbances elsewhere—like adding a large number of people near the scheduled completion date.

That's why you need system models. Models expose and explain the non-linear system dynamics so you can start doing something about your back problems before you actually start experiencing the pain. Or your project before you actually start experience the crisis.

## 5.6. Helpful Hints and Suggestions

• The most important thing about the diagram of effects is not the diagram, but the diagramming. When developing a diagram of effects to understand what is going on in a project, it's best to develop diagrams in a group, and listen to the discussion that emerges. For instance, you might listen for hesitations, disagreements, and expressions of surprise. Hesitations might indicate lack of understanding of an effect. Disagreements might indicate more than one effect, with some people noticing one and some noticing another. Surprise might indicate that some managers have been overlooking this effect.

• Don't get into arguments about what to include on the graph. At first, include everything. Later, you can exclude factors that don't contribute to non-linearities. For control purposes, non-linearities will generally dominate linear effects, and so can often be ignored in real project planning after you've completed the diagram and identified all the non-linear effects. But you'll want to retain any effect that's part of a feedback loop, as we'll see in the next chapter.

• For most people, mathematical models of systems dynamics are not easy to use or understand, but for some people, such models are a natural medium for communication. When making a mathematical model, we start by translating a diagram of effects into a set of equations. The arrow is replaced by the "=" sign, so for each node with at least one arrow entering, we get an equation with that node's measurement on the left-hand side, as in

Relative progress = f()

This says that relative progress depends on some other measurements, which can be determined by the source of each arrow entering the relative progress node. Thus, we know that

Relative progress = f(productive work finished, amount of work to be done)

In this case, we know by the definition of relative progress that the function, f, is a simple division:

Relative progress = Productive work finished / Amount of

work to be done

The gray dot indicates that the effects are in opposite directions, and sure enough, dividing by "amount of work to be done" means that the more work to be done, the less relative progress. Thus, the dot translates into some mathematical operation that reverses effects, such as division or subtraction.

In other cases, we may have to make measurements to determine the form of the equation. For instance, we might measure a number of projects that added people and discover that a good estimate of coordination labor for the first 4 weeks is,

Coordination required = (5.5 hours/week) x (New people added)2

If you are interested in this level of numerical description of many of the effects relationships in software development, see Boehm's Software Engineering Economics.

When all affected boxes have been thus translated, we have a set of equations representing the same system represented by the diagram. They might all be linear equations (in which case it is called a "linear system"), or some might be non-linear. They might be algebraic, differential, or integro-differential equations. They might be discrete or continuous equations (in which case we have a "discrete" or a "continuous" system). Regardless of their final form, their development starts from the same diagram of effects. Only the solution methods will differ.

### 5.7. Summary

1. Every manager and programmer has models of how things work in their software pattern, though many models are implicit in their behavior, rather than stated explicitly. Things go awry in software projects because people are unable to face reality and because they use incorrect system models.

2. Linear models are attractive because of additivity. Linear systems are easier to model, easier to predict, and easier to control. Managers often commit scaling fallacies because linear models are so attractive.

3. The diagram of effects is a tool for helping model system dynamics to reveal non-linearities. Being a two-dimensional picture, it is more suited than verbal descriptions to the job of describing non-linear systems.

4. One way of developing a diagram of effects is to start with the output—the variable whose behavior you wish to control. You then brainstorm and chart backwards effects from that variable— other variables that could affect it. From these, you chart backwards again, unveiling secondary effects, which you can trace through the primary effects to the variable of interest. You may want to explicitly indicate multiplicative effects because of their importance.

5. Non-linearity is the reason things go awry, so searching for non-linearity is a major task of system modeling.

## 5.8. Practice

1. The elliptical cloud indicates a clear measurement, but often measurements are not as clear as they seem (which will be one subject covered in the following volume). For instance, "Weight" (in Figure 5-4) could mean several things, such as,

a. the weight seen on a scale

b. an average of several scale weights over some period of time

c. perceived weight, according to tightness of clothing

d. fat weight vs. muscle weight

Each of these measures might have a different dynamic in the weight-exercise-back pain system. Sketch at least one effects dynamic for each of the four alternatives.

3. Another choice for the Weight node might be "Change in Weight." At the level of the diagram of effects, there's no difference between the two, but if you favor mathematical models, you'll see that the two views will produce different types of equations. Explain this difference. Then try to explain it to someone without mathematical training to the level of differential equations.

2. In the Brooks's Law dynamic (Figure 5-1), "productive work finished" could be interpreted and measured in several ways. List at least three different interpretations. Sketch at least one effects dynamic for each of the alternative interpretations.

146

# Chapter 6: Feedback Effects

*Don't you think you'd be safer down on the ground?" Alice went on, not with any idea of making another riddle, but simply in her good-natured anxiety for the queer creature. The wall is so very narrow!"*

*"What tremendously easy riddles you ask!" Humpty Dumpty growled out. "Of course I don't think so! Why, if ever I did fall off—which there's no chance of—but if I did—" Here he pursed up his lips, and looked so solemn and grand that Alice could hardly help laughing. "If I did fall," he went on. "the King has promised me—ah, you may turn pale, if you like! You didn't think I was going to say that, did you? The King has promised me—with his very own mouth—to—to—"*

*"To send all his horses and all his men," Alice interrupted, rather unwisely.*

If you don't pay attention to the system dynamics, and wait, instead, until the curves of Figure 5-5 are clearly distinguishable, you will pay a lot greater price in pain and suffering before you finally solve the problem. Even with all this pain and suffering, however, the model of Figure 5-4 says you could still reverse the course of your back crisis, even though the price will be high. Sometimes, however, an action cannot easily be reversed, in spite of all the promises of help from higher management.

## 6.1 The Humpty Dumpty Syndrome

In the thirty years since I started using *Alice* as my guiding text for software engineering, I've witnessed the following sequence at least 200 times:

1. A project manager (Humpty) becomes aware that he is sitting on a very narrow ledge of some sort.

2. Humpty goes to his manager and tells about his anxieties.

3. Humpty's manager says, "Don't worry, that's not going to happen. But, if it *did* happen, I'll bail you out with lots of resources. The only thing is, you must not go around talking about this situation, or people will be alarmed (including *my* manager)."

4. Humpty goes back and keeps his mouth shut. He is able to keep his mouth shut by convincing himself that nothing is really going to happen.

5. Sometimes things do get better by themselves. More often, things go non-linear and the Humpty has egg all over his face. Humpty's manager may initially support him with lots of resources, but finally needs a scapegoat because things can't be put back together again. Guess who he chooses!

One variation of this Humpty Dumpty Syndrome is when a consultant (Alice) comes along in the middle of the process and tries to explain things to Humpty. Alice is powerless to *explain* why she's so worried, and Humpty is skilled at not facing reality. I recommend that you study the original to learn all the devices that Humpty uses to keep himself from listening to Alice.

The Humpty Dumpty Syndrome is probably what Brooks had in mind when he said that "software managers lack the personal effectiveness to be 'courteously stubborn.'" In this chapter, we'll arm software managers with a tool for courteous stubbornness. With diagrams of effects, they'll be able to describe convincingly those system dynamics too strong to be reversed—no matter what the King promises.

## 6.2 Runaway, Explosion and Collapse

The idea that you can always revoke previous actions is based on two fallacies, the "Reversible Fallacy" and the "Causation Fallacy." Figure 6-1 shows another possible analysis of the back pain crisis, an analysis that does not allow you simply to reverse your troubles after you reach a given point.

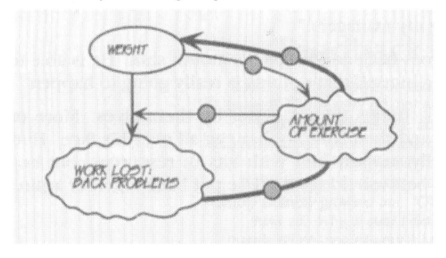

**Figure 6-1. A feedback model of the relationship between weight and the frequency of lower back crises.**

### 6.2.1. The Reversible Fallacy

The Reversible Fallacy says,

What is done can always be undone.

If this were true, management would be a lot easier. If a control action didn't work out right, you could just go back to where you were by reversing that action. For instance, if you get a back spasm from lifting a heavy rock, you can just stop lifting the rock and the spasm will go away. Similarly, if you lost your temper and fired half the staff, you could correct your mistake by hiring them back the next day. Neither backs nor employees are as reversible as that. What is done *cannot* always be undone.

### 6.2.2. The Causation Fallacy

The Causation Fallacy says:

Every effect has a cause,…and we can tell which is which.

That seems true enough in Figure 5-4, but the model of Figure 6-1 recognizes that causality is not always a one-way street. Not only does decreased exercise lead to greater frequency of back pain, but the more your back hurts, the less likely you are to exercise. Moreover, if you exercise less while eating the same amount, you will gain weight. Adding these two effects to the diagram leads to three *feedback cycles* in the model (Figure 6-2):

1. back problems→less exercise→back problems
2. less exercise→increased weight →less exercise
3. back problems→less exercise→increased weight →back

problems

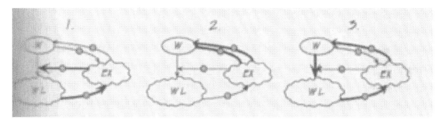

**Figure 6-2. Three different feedback cycles in the weight-back problems-exercise diagram of Figure 6-1 , shown by the paths traced in darker arrows.**

Feedback cycles like these produce a strikingly different system dynamic than we have seen so far—a dynamic in which cause and effect cannot be separated. Cycles 1 and 2 are direct, and cycle 3 is less direct, but all three cycles are what we call *positive feedback loops*. We can determine that they are positive feedback loops by tracing (multiplying) the dots along a path back to the beginning of the path. An even number of dots around the cycle means the loop is positive—or "self-reinforcing," or "deviation-amplifying," to use some other common terms.

For instance, weight increases back problems, which decrease exercise, which increases weight, so that in the end, *weight increases weight*. Or *back problems increase back problems*. Or *less exercise leads to even less exercise*. So, does gaining weight cause back problems, or do back problems cause gaining weight? So much for the Causation Fallacy.

### 6.2.3. Irreversiblity: explosion or collapse

151

Positive feedback—X increases X—is the recipe for explosion or collapse. Explosion and a collapse are both "runaway" conditions. The difference between them *simply depends on the way you name the variables you are measuring*. In the system of Figure 6-1, weight will explode, exercise will collapse, time lost to back problems will explode—and your back itself will probably collapse. Figure 6-3 shows a graph of the explosion of back problems—or the collapse of your back—comparing two models. The simple multiplicative model may initially look more severe than the feedback model, but the nature of feedback is that its non-linearities are ultimately much more powerful. Eventually, the feedback curve shoots up and explodes off the scale of the graph.

Of course, work lost from back pain cannot actually grow infinitely, because nothing can grow infinitely. For instance, when you reach 100% lost working time, you will cross a threshold and the system of Figure 6-1 will "break." In other words, something so big will happen that the old model will no longer apply. Unlike the multiplicative non-linearity of Figure 5-4, the non-linearity of Figure 6-1 becomes *irreversible*. No matter how much we are willing to pay, it's never going to be the same old Humpty Dumpty.

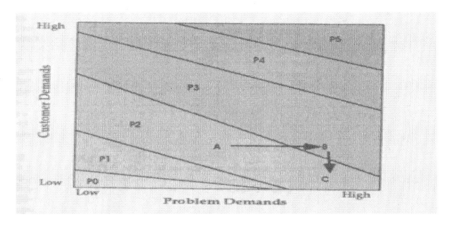

**Figure 6-3. A graph of the feedback model's prediction of the relationship between weight and the frequency of lower back crises.**

For instance, when back pain causes you to miss 100% of your work, may lose your job, or be forced to go on disability leave. Even worse, the collapse might lead you to the point where you must have back surgery. As anyone knows who has ever experienced back surgery, you're grateful for the relief (if the surgery was a success), but you're never be quite the same as you were before you started on this runaway path.

## 6.3. Act Early, Act Small

Because of positive feedback cycles, back injuries are not reversible, and that's why doctors recommend a regime of weight reduction and curative exercise *from the moment you experience the first symptoms of back problems.* Patients are often foolishly optimistic — "it can't happen to me" — but doctors know from long

153

experience with back system dynamics that their back won't get better "by itself."

### 6.3.1 Brooks's Law made worse by management action

The same is true in software engineering systems. As Brooks observed, managers are often foolishly optimistic about things going well. Moreover, when things do go poorly, they imagine that they will get better "by themselves." If Pattern 2 managers do realize there's a problem, they don't know how to reason about it, or communicate about it, so they slip into the Humpty Dumpty Syndrome, which delays action even further. Then, when they finally do realize that their non-linear system doesn't "fix itself," they may attempt too big a correction—landing on the project with both feet, starting an even worse non-linear cycle.

Figure 6-4 shows a more complete Brooks's Law dynamic, including a causal (darkened) line from Relative progress back to addition of new people. Notice how we have collapsed several nodes to eliminate details that are not essential to understanding this dynamic. This is similar to the collapse of detail in software design drawings or data flow diagrams, a technique that should be familiar to most readers.

The new feedback line converts a mild multiplicative non-linearity (like the two lines going into "relative progress" in Figure 6-3) into a full-blown positive feedback loop (involving the dark line in Figure 6-3). Instead of merely making the project late, a sufficiently foolish manager can make the project totally collapse.

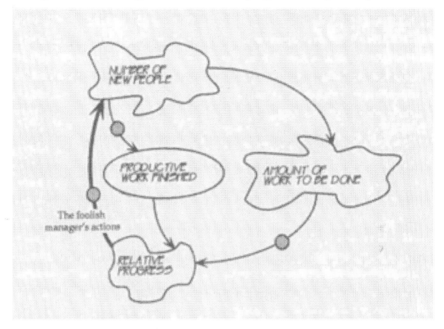

**Figure 6-4. The foolish manager's actions convert a mildly non-linear dynamic into a full-blown positive feedback dynamic.**

### 6.3.2 The Generalized Brooks's Law

This effect of management actions actually producing collapse of a project is so common in Pattern 2 organizations that it is worthy of a name. I call it the "Generalized Brooks's Law" because it includes Brooks's original law as a special case. Figure 6-5 shows the generalized diagram of effects for Brooks's Law.

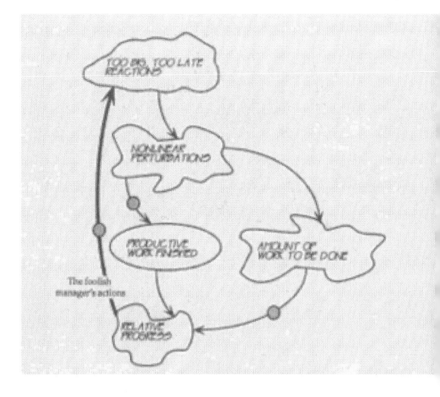

**Figure 6-5. The Generalized Brooks's Law, with management reacting as relative progress grows worse, but reacting too late, and too large, thus creating a non-linear positive feedback dynamic.**

Notice that in the generalized law, the manager introduces non-linearities in at least three different ways:

1. by feeding back back changes that contribute to the workload

2. by feeding back back changes that diminish the effective workforce

156

3. by waiting so long to make these changes that they have no chance of being effective unless they are big, and through this bigness creating other non-linear effects within the project system.

These actions will be all too familiar to anyone who has ever worked in a Pattern 2 organization.

## 6.4. Negative Feedback—Why Everything Doesn't Collapse

With all the positive feedback loops in the world, why doesn't everything collapse? Why don't some people *ever* have a back crisis? Isn't their system model the same as ours? Although their model may be the same as the model of Figure 6-1, they probably run the feedback loops *in reverse*. For them, exercise keeps weight down, which keeps back problems down, which leaves them free to exercise, which keeps weight down. This leads not to a collapse of the *back*, but to a "collapse" of back *problems*—a runaway to zero. This seems a salubrious result, but because of the way the system is constructed, there are hazards lurking in the shadows.

### 6.4.1 A system waiting for a disaster to happen

Because of these positive feedback loops, the model of Figure 6-1 is *unstable*. It may not be collapsing now, but it's just waiting for a runaway to happen in one direction or another—although a "runaway" to no back problems may be a very desirable condition. The same cycle as the one producing gross overweight can produce problems like anorexia, all depending on how the cycle gets

157

started. In reality, of course, there must be other factors that come into play before *weight* collapses to zero—total starvation and death.

When you analyze a software development organization, one of the first things you must do is look for positive feedback loops —disasters waiting to happen, like Humpty Dumpty sitting on a narrow ledge. Unless these unstable systems are stabilized in some way, all other management actions are merely cosmetic.

### 6.4.2 Negative feedback loops

There are many factors capable of stabilizing a dynamic system, and many cosmetic actions that can delay the inevitable. A back brace may allow you to keep on working for a week or so until a project is completed. At the same time, it weakens the muscles in your back so that if a disaster does come, it will be much worse. It also can give you a false sense of confidence, causing you to postpone actions that could prevent disaster in the long run.

In the same way, throwing lots of overtime hours into testing a bug-ridden system may delay the disaster for a short time, perhaps even long enough to get a shippable product. But—as we shall see later—it's likely to lead to a more complete and irreversible system collapse.

In the long run, only certain actions have the power to prevent collapse. In particular, only *other feedback loops* have the power to consistently offset the power of positive feedback loops. In living systems, there are often dozens or hundreds of such loops acting to regulate the essential variables of life, which is why life can be highly stable, even in a highly unstable environment. Each of these stabilizing loops are "negative feedback loops," or "deviation-reducing processes."

When listening to management proposals for correcting an unstable software project, I always check these proposals for negative feedback loops that will regulate the essential project variables. For instance, lots of overtime does add some feedback loops, but they are all positive, and thus will worsen the situation. On the other hand, properly conducted technical reviews can participate in a number of negative feedback loops that may help get things under control.

### 6.4.3 How feedback loops regulate

Figure 6-6 shows one such feedback loop in the weight-back pain system. The amount you eat obviously has a positive effect on your weight. This model says that if your back hurts enough, you may lose your appetite and reduce your food intake. Tracing the loop of

*more back problems→less eating→decreased weight →fewer back problems*

shows that an *more back problems tends to lead to fewer back problems*. Also, more weight tends to lead to less weight, and more work lost tends to lead to less work lost. Unlike the positive feedback loops, this negative feedback loop will tend to have a stabilizing effect on all variables in the system.

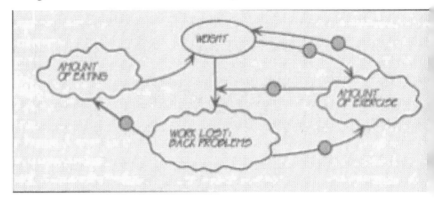

**Figure 6-6. A negative feedback loop added to the positive feedback model of the relationship between weight and the frequency of lower back crises. Amount of eating is reduced in the face of lost work due to back problems.**

If you examine our original feedback model of controlling a software development system, redrawn as Figure 6-7, you'll now recognize that there are two main feedback loops connecting controller and development system. This model of control is effective only if at least one of the feedback loops containing controller and system is negative. Deviations from the desired course of development events must lead to feedback of actions that diminish those deviations, thus stabilizing the system. For instance,

• Schedule slippage could lead to reduced requirements.

• More errors could lead to more resources devoted to technical reviews.

• People falling ill could lead to reduction of scheduled overtime.

• Poor customer acceptance could lead to additional design training.

• Any of the above could lead to additional management training.

On the other hand, you'll recognize that this same diagram could also model *positive* feedback such as the Generalized Brooks's Law. If the controller does the wrong thing—like adding workers late in the project in an attempt to reduce schedule slippage—then the situation will get worse. In fact, the controller's wrong actions could turn even a relatively benign linear system into a raging non-linear one (as in Figure 6-4)—and software development systems are decidedly not benign linear systems, for reasons we shall soon discover.

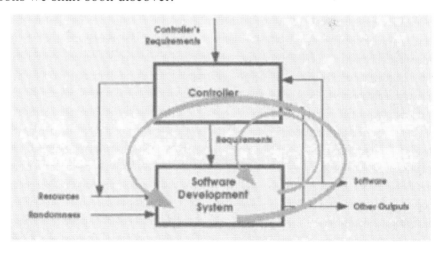

**Figure 6-7. The Pattern 3 model of controlling a software development contains two feedback loops connecting Controller and System—one through resources and one through Requirements. In a Pattern 2 organization, either of these often turns out to be positive.**

### 6.5. Helpful Hints and Suggestions

• In Figure 6-4, we collapsed some of the detail out of our original Brooks's Law figure. This is an alternative way to develop diagrams of effects, the first way being output to input. You may wish to use this approach when you are dealing with general problems, such as the overall design of a new development or maintenance process. Start with the big variables and begin connecting them according to their effects. To determine what those effects might be, explode each variable into a more detailed diagram of effects.

• A third way to develop diagrams of effects is to move from input to output. This is an approach to use when you are considering some action to improve one variable but first want to examine how the action might impact other variables—thus avoiding one of the traps of the Generalized Brooks's Law. You start with the variables you will change and work *forward* to other variables that they will affect (which might include feedback effects to themselves, perhaps counteracting what you are trying to do.) You stop when the moving forward yields no new variables.

• "Act early; act small" is a crucial maxim for Pattern 3

managers, and can also be used to guide management training. To act early, you must sharpen your powers of observation. To act small, you must sharpen your understanding of the subtleties of human behavior.

• Negative feedback isn't always desirable, because stability isn't always desirable. When you are trying to get an organization to change its pattern, you will encounter a large number of negative feedback loops that work to keep it from changing. To accomplish change, you will have to establish some positive feedback loops that tend to make the system "run away" to the new pattern. Before you can do this, however, you'll need a solid understanding of stabilizing loops.

### 6.6. Summary

1. The Humpty Dumpty Syndrome explains one reason why project managers are unable to be courteously stubborn to their mangers, and what happens as a result.

2. Projects run away—explode or collapse—because managers believe two fallacies: The Reversible Fallacy (that actions can always be undone) and The Causation Fallacy (that every cause has one effect, and you can tell which is cause and which is effect.)

3. One reason management action contributes to runaway is the tendency to respond too late to deviations, which then forces

management to big actions which themselves have non-linear consequences. That's why it's necessary to "act early; act small."

3. The effect of Brooks's Law can be made worse by management action. Moreover, the same pattern of management action can lead to a Generalized Brooks's Law, which shows how management action is often the leading cause of project collapse.

4. One reason management action contributes to runaway is the tendency to respond too late to deviations, which then forces management to big actions which themselves have non-linear consequences. That's why it's necessary to "act early; act small."

5. Negative feedback is the only mechanism that has the speed and power to prevent runaway due to positive feedback loops in a system. The Pattern 3 controller has two major negative feedback loops with which to exercise control—one involving resources and one involving requirements.

### 6.7. Practice

1. For the mathematically inclined, show why the equations derived from positive feedback loops lead to runaway conditions, using the method of translating diagrams of effects into equations given in the previous chapter. Explain your reasoning to someone without your mathematical background. Do you resort to diagrams? Did they understand?

2. Give three other examples of negative feedback actions a controller can exercise through the requirements loop of Figure 6-7. Give three examples that can be exercised through the resources loop.

3. What other negative feedback loops could you construct to stabilize the system of Figure 6-1?

4. What other negative feedback loops could you construct to stabilize the system of Figure 6-5, the Generalization of Brooks Law?

5. What positive feedback loops could you construct to destabilize your own organization and drive it toward a new pattern?

# Chapter 7: Steering Software

*"It is completely unimportant. That is why it is so interesting."* Agatha Christie

In 1989, Watts Humphrey of the Software Engineering Institute was interviewed by the IEEE about SEI's 5-level process-maturity model. He said, "Although the SEI has found several projects at level 3, no company surpassed the second level." In this chapter, we'll examine one of the major barriers to the transition to level 3 (or Pattern 3, as we prefer to call it). That barrier is the characteristic idea that binds managers to Pattern 2:

Pattern 2: "It's possible to make a project plan and follow it exactly."

We'll also look at what you need to free yourself from Pattern 2 thinking, the characteristic idea of Pattern 3:

Pattern 3: "Plans are rough guides. We need steering to stay on course."

## 7.1. Methodologies and Feedback Control

Even with the most accurate models, we won't always be successful at controlling every aspect of software projects, if only because of the randomness of the project's input. Nevertheless, meaningful measurement based on accurate effects models will lead us to make successful predictions more frequently than simple extrapolation would allow. But in order to *steer*, you need more than predictions of how the system will behave by itself. You also need *models of how their intervention will affect the system* they're trying to control. But, if you believe that plans can be followed exactly, you'll also believe that you're wasting your time modeling interventions—because in your mind, they will never be required.

### 7.1.1 Plans: the great contribution of Pattern 2

Plans for orderly software development are the great achievement of organizations arriving at Pattern 2. Individual organizations, as well as consulting organizations serving hundreds of organizations, have made major efforts to prescribe and document sequences of actions needed to control software. Integrated sets of these actions are often packaged and sold as "methodologies."

A typical methodology is a process that prescribes an ideal series of steps that will take your project from beginning to end. A simple methodology might start with a feasibility study, then do requirements, then high-level design, then detailed-design, then code, then unit test, then system test, then beta-test, then product release. Figure 7-1 shows the "Waterfall Process Model," an early model still followed by many organizations—either Pattern 2 or, more likely, Pattern 1 trying to become Pattern 2.

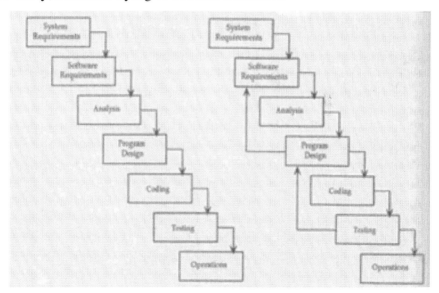

**Figure 7-1. (on the left)The Waterfall Process Model is essentially a sequence of steps—a program for human and machine activities. Note that this is not a diagram of effects, but a process model. The nodes don't represent measurements, but activities to be done. The arrows can be translated into the words "followed by."**

**Figure 7-2. (on the right) Modified Waterfall Process Models were early attempts to indicate non-linear possibilities through (ideally negative) feedback loops.**

The original Waterfall Process Model is strictly a sequential plan, with the arrows between nodes translating into the words "followed by." After a number of years, modified Waterfall models began to appear, such as shown in Figure 7-2. The backward arrows are sometimes referred to as "feedback" arrows, but this use of the term doesn't correspond to the conventional use in control theory. A better reading of these arrows is "sometimes followed by a return to." In programming terms, these arrows are backward GOTOs.

These backward arrows were a form of recognition that a purely linear process was not an adequate description for what really goes on in a software development process. But they lead to poor estimating, which is a major cause of schedule overruns.

### 7.1.2 Why pure sequential methods don't always work

Here's a riddle. Many projects follow these sequential methodologies with great success, but other organizations can't seem to make them work. Why?

Before answering this riddle, consider this parable:

The first time my colleague, Don Gause, came to visit my house in the country, I gave him the following set of instructions over the phone:

      1. At Greenwood exit, leave Interstate 80 and go south 11 miles.

      2. At the T, take Highway US 34 west.

      3. When you reach Eagle, continue west 3 miles to 176th Street.

      4. Turn south on 176th Street (a dirt road) and go .6 miles.

      5. You will see a white house on the right, which is our house.

These seem simple enough, but Don left out the decimal point in step 4. After driving 6 miles (and an extra 2 miles for good measure) South, he couldn't find any white house on either side of 176th Street . He searched in various ways for over an hour (after all, he had a reputation as a problem-solver to uphold), he finally gave up and called me for further instructions.

Think of this as a metaphor for developing software under the direction of a sequential methodology. My instructions to Don were indeed an ideal set of instructions from an unknown spot on Interstate to Jerry's house. This method is completely linear *unless*

*Don makes a mistake*. Once the mistake is made, there is no provision for correction, no method describing what to do next.

My assumption was much like the assumptions underlying sequential methodologies for software development:

1. There would be no mistakes.

2. If there happened to be any mistakes, they would be little ones.

3. The responsible parties would certainly know how to correct such little mistakes.

This, then, is the answer to my riddle: sequential methodologies are essentially linear processes, supplemented by *implicit* feedback. If nothing goes too far wrong, reasonable people can feed back small linear corrections, and that's the ideal way for a project to work. But things don't always happen that way, and sometimes a project gets thwacked by something decidedly non-linear.

At the point when *even one* measurement in an effects diagram becomes non-linear, the project's controller needs to know how to make appropriate non-linear corrections—or at least not unknowingly contribute to the non-linearity. Some managers make appropriate corrections instinctively, but as projects grow more complex, instinct falters. That's why we need *explicit* models of controller's interventions—guides to steering.

170

### 7.1.3 Methodologies can discourage innovation

There's a more subtle reason why sequential methodologies fail, as suggested by yet another metaphor—the "Triptik," a trip guide issued by the American Automobile Association (AAA) to its members (see Figure 7-3 for an example).

Some years ago, Dani and I were driving to a meeting of the American Anthropological Association (also AAA), using the plan provided in Triptik form by the other AAA. We had stopped to visit our friend, Jim Fleming, in Columbus, Indiana. As we started out of Columbus on State Highway 7 to Interstate 65, we saw a sign pointing down County Road 46 to the town of Gnaw Bone.

Now, I had always been fascinated that there was a place called Gnaw Bone, but never dreamed I'd have a chance to actually experience being there. Dani, however, was reluctant to go out of our way. I tried to encourage her by pointing out that the black dots along County Road 46, which indicated a scenic route. That proved to be a mistake.

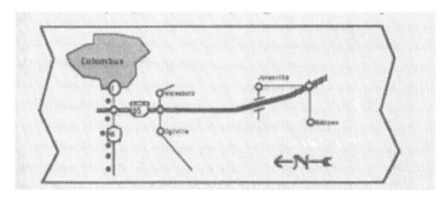

**Figure 7-3. A small segment of a AAA Triptik that Dani and Jerry were using to find their way to the AAA meeting.**

"Look," she said. "The Triptik doesn't indicate how we would get back on 65. Do we come to Ogilville, head for Jonesville, or just look for Bobtown? We might not be able to get to any of those places—look how the Jonesville road passes under the Interstate. We could be going a hundred miles out of our way."

"Oh, it couldn't be that far," I argued.

"We don't have a state map, so how can you be so sure? I definitely don't want to get lost in Brown County and miss the start of my meeting."

Because we used a narrow linear map, I never got to explore the fascinating town of Gnaw Bone. In a similar fashion, Pattern 2 organizations who use narrow sequential methodologies often fail to explore the territory around their chosen route to project success. Or, when they do explore, the often get lost and fail to arrive on schedule. As Humphrey says,

Unless they are introduced with great care, new tools and methods will affect the process, thus destroying the relevance of the intuitive historical base on which the organization relies. Without a defined process framework in which to address these risks, it is even possible for a new technology to do more harm than good.

This possibility—"getting lost without a wide scale map"—is

another reason why Pattern 2 organizations tend to be so conservative about innovations. Given what they know, it's *smart* to be conservative.

### 7.1.4 Adding feedback to the methodology

More sophisticated methodologies, like the Waterfall Model in Figure 7-2, do attempt to deal with the possibility of non-linear deviations by providing for feedback. Notice how some kind of feedback is indicated in that diagram:

1. from the program design stage to the software requirements stage

2. from the testing stage to the program design stage

These arrows in a process diagram say, in effect, "under some circumstances we will go back and do this step over." In my experience, they don't mean much in practice because:

1. There are many, many places besides the end of a "phase" when the controller gets information saying that the project is off the course. These deviations may seem "completely unimportant. That is why it is so interesting." They are exactly the things real controllers need to notice if they are to "act early, act small."

2. Getting back on course by recreating a design or a specification is such an enormous piece of work to do over that it's always a non-linear disturbance.

3. Besides, redoing a design or specification is such an

enormous piece of work that managers seldom dare to actually do them over, lest they get lost in downtown Gnaw Bone.

4. The methodology doesn't provide any sense of what *information* is to be fed back from one stage to the other, so people don't really have a map of what they're supposed to do.

5. The methodology doesn't say anything about the dozens or hundreds of other feedback situations or how to handle them. The basic focus seems to dictate a choice, "either do it right or do it completely over (presumably right the next time)." The methodology makes no small distinctions or corrections between doing it right and doing it wrong.

### 7.1.5 Keeping the feedback early and small

Recent authors have attempted to correct some of these problems by creating smaller feedback loops in their methodology. For instance, Humphrey introduces the valuable idea of "basic unit cells" (Figure 7-4) from which a larger process can be composed. Each of these basic unit cells has feedback in from later cells and back to earlier cells. By making these cells smaller, the non-linearity is hopefully minimized.

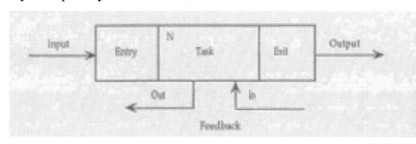

**Figure 7-4. By building processes from basic unit cells, Humphrey adds smaller scale feedback to a large scale development process, thus creating a more stable process.**

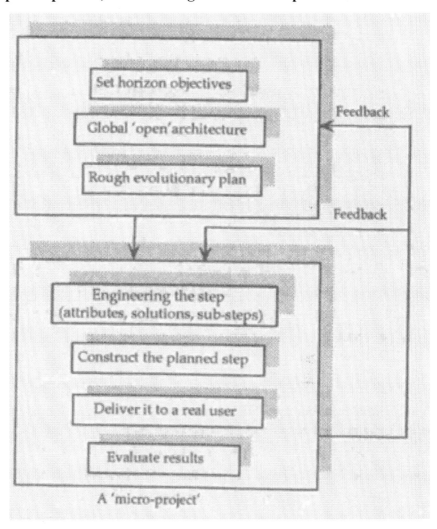

**Figure 7-5. By building the entire product in small evolutionary units, Gilb ensures that feedback cycles must be shorter in time and smaller in impact.**

Another approach—which can be used in conjunction with Humphrey's basic unit cells—is Gilb's "Evolutionary Delivery Cycle." As shown in Figure 7-5, work is done in "micro-projects," so that feedback cycles cannot grow too large or too big. At most, feedback can move from one micro-project to the next.

Humphrey and Gilb are just two of many examples illustrating that methodologists are becoming aware of the importance of feedback. I recommend you examine their important work, but I will not explore it further here because all such software methodology work still omits most of the important available feedback.

### 7.1.5 Applying the feedback at different levels

Both basic unit cells and micro-projects address the problem of feedback, but still focus only on the *product* being built. The feedback they us is information about the product, not information about the process in general. An effective manager needs to know much more information, much earlier, than the product alone can provide.

A more general focus is on the *process*, as taught by Deming and others (Figure 7-6). In effect, these efforts use define where they are and where they desire to go in terms of the *process*, not the product. In other words, the process *is* their product, and is controlled by the same sort of feedback dynamics. An ideal improvement program combines this focus with the idea of small size improvements to achieve successful change with a minimum of instability.

As we'll see later, this approach can also be carried out at the *cultural* level, above the level of particular processes, let alone products. Wherever we look, people are discovering that the same control model is needed at all levels, and with it, the ability to think and observe in terms of non-linear effects and then to act in concordance with those observations and thoughts.

Figure 7-6. By focusing on the process, Hewlett-Packard and other firms have been able to establish great gains in software quality and productivity. The cycle of process improvement is just like a product improvement cycle, but *the process is the product*.

## 7.2. The Human Decision Point

Models are always approximations, so none of them is ever "perfect"—but they all should be *believable*. To use models effectively, we must be able to act *as if* we believe them, even while we remember that they are approximations.

We get into serious trouble with models when we *do* believe them. In particular, when a model says, or implies, that some action is impossible, we are not likely to consider attempting that action. Good intervention models will help us to understand what we can't control, but a faulty model may lead us to overlook a number of effective interventions. In this section, we'll examine how these oversights can happen.

### 7.2.1 Intervention models and invisible states

An intervention model says something like this (where B is the "bad" state I'm trying to change , and G is the "good" state I'm trying to attain):

> If the system is in state B,
>
> and I do X,
>
> then Y will happen
>
> (which is hopefully closer to G).

To take a simple example, the waterfall model of Figure 7-2 says that

> If the program design is finished (state B)
>
> and we do the coding (X)
>
> then we will be in the testing state (Y)
>
> (which is hopefully closer to G)

Given the particular model, there's no suggestion that something that happens in coding might send the project further away from G, to some place such as:

1. a previous step in the methodology, such as, back to software requirements

2. a state not mentioned in the methodology, such as, a state where

a. there are large numbers of difficult coding errors

b. project members are falsely confident

c. upper management wrongly believes the project is closer to completion

d. one of the key programmers has gotten sick from overwork

e. a programmer and a team lead have become bitter enemies.

Software people are perhaps too familiar with methodologies (which are models of processes) and not familiar enough with effects models. This is one reason they're not very good at predicting the effects that are not directly based on the states of their methodology. Figure 7-7 is intended to clarify the distinction.

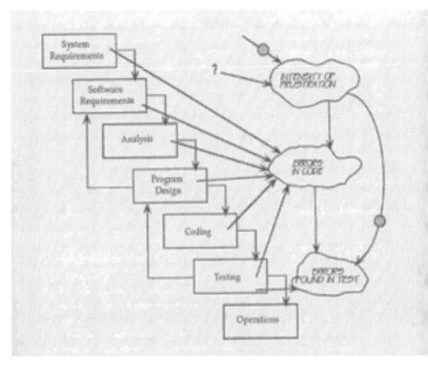

**Figure 7-7. The difference between a process model and a diagram of effects is shown by this diagram of the Waterfall Model showing where some measurements might originate. The feeling of frustration might not originate in a specific step that we could identify in the Waterfall Model, but still be a critical variable in the project's success.**

In the figure, we have superimposed on the Feedback Waterfall Model some measurements from a diagram of effects:

1. *Errors found in test* is certainly associated with one and only one stage in the process model, but may be *influenced* by other variables seemingly not related to that stage. For example, the *intensity of the feeling of frustration* throughout the project may

lessen the effectiveness of the testing effort.

2. *Errors in code* could be associated with any stage in the methodology, because they could originate anywhere, perhaps including places not mentioned in the methodology itself, such as someone from a different project corrupting the source code data base. They may also be influenced by other variables, such as the feeling of frustration.

3. Variables such as *the intensity of the feeling of frustration* may be influenced by any number of factors. We may have a hard time identifying these effects. Although we generally won't be able to associate such variables with any particular stage in the Waterfall Model, that doesn't diminish their importance. If anything, it increases them.

In other words, the variables used by a controller may be connected with the product (which is the ultimate interest) or simply be some of the "other outputs" we saw way back in Figure 4-4. If you look again at that figure, you'll notice (as you may not have noticed before) that the controller takes input from *both* the software and the other outputs. But most methodologies are so product focused that they never mention other outputs not *directly* connected with product quality, cost, or schedule.

To a great extent, managing to avoid a crisis consists of recognizing, nurturing, strengthening, and creating stabilizing feedback loops, then sitting back and letting them do the work of preventing collapse. It also depends on recognizing, discouraging, negating, and decoupling positive feedback loops, such as blindly adding more workers late in the project might do. Only by modeling your interventions can you avoid creating new positive feedback loops in your efforts to solve the problems created by old ones. If your process model doesn't even acknowledge the existence of certain states, it has no chance of guiding you to effective interventions.

### 7.2.2 Visualizing the invisible

I once was called to a consult on a troubled project that was missing all its goals, much to the puzzlement of its project manger, Simon. As part of my visit, I attended a code review meeting which (against my advice) Simon also attended. Herb, whose code was being reviewed, took a lot of personal abuse from Simon, to the point where his eyes started watering. I called for a "health break," and during the break, Simon came up to me and asked, "Does Herb have something in his eye?"

"Why do you ask?" I replied.

"Well, I noticed that there was water coming out of his eye."

After studying the project, I came to the conclusion that the project was in trouble largely because almost all of the people were feeling totally discounted by their management. In Simon's model of the world, emotional states of people in his project simply didn't exist. If they had been visible, Simon would have seen there was trouble early, and been able to act small to do something about it. Therefore, I could explain nothing to Simon until he learned some new models, so he could see what was previously invisible.

If you are managing a software project and are considering an intervention to control something, you must first express your idea in terms of the intervention model by answering the following questions:

1. What is the state of the system now (B)?

2. What is the action I intend to take (X)?

3. What will be the dynamic of a system in state B if I take the action X?

4. Is Y (where the dynamic will take the system) closer to G?

To answer these questions, you probably need methods of making visible that which has previously been invisible.

## 7.3 It's Not The Event That Counts, It's Your Reaction To The Event

Feedback loops in action sometimes seem to have a "mind of their own." That's because managers are blind to the key role that people—especially management people—play in each feedback.

All of the loops that concern management contain *decisions by people*.

Whenever there's a human decision point in the system,

It's not the event that determines the next event,

but someone's reaction to that event.

For some Pattern 2 readers, this maxim will be the hardest to swallow of all the ideas in this book. They would like to believe that projects obey some set of mechanical laws, like Newton's Laws of Motion, and that the manager's job is to learn these laws, set up the project properly, and then let nature take its course to success. This is an especially comforting idea to those managers who are afraid of their own workers, because it means that they can hide in their offices and manipulate plans, rather than deal with real human beings. As long as they deny the role of human action in project management, they'll never be successful project managers.

The human decision points in our model *must* be identified because *they're the places where we have a chance to prevent a crisis*. When Fred Brooks says, "More software projects have gone awry for lack of calendar time than for all other causes combined," he could have said, "More software projects have gone awry *because their managers didn't know how to respond to lack of calendar time...*" We'll never have complete control, but neither are we victims.

Of course, every system does have some "laws of nature" that we can't do anything directly about. In the back pain system, if we eat more, we'll gain weight—that's a *physiological* law. It's also a physiological law that if we gain weight, we're more likely to have back pain. To manage back pain, we need to learn which relationships we *can* influence, and then act on them. For instance, there's no natural law that says "When you're in pain, eat something." Your mother may have taught you that, but grown-ups don't have to do what their mothers taught them.

You could *decide* to do what your mother said and increase your eating in response to the pain, thus converting a possibly stabilizing loop into another force for destabilizing. But you do have choices as to how back pain will affect your eating and exercise habits, and how your weight will affect your exercise. Therefore, you could just as well decide to *decrease* your eating when your back hurts, as many people do. Figure 7-8 shows Figure 6-6 redrawn to identify those effects lines that are within your control.

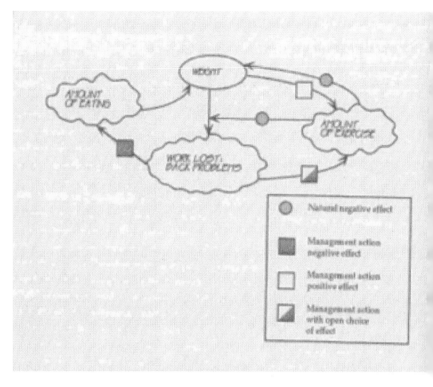

**Figure 7-8. Figure 6-6 redrawn to emphasize those effects that are human decisions (positive or negative). Reversing certain "natural" decisions produces a more stable, healthier system.**

The lines are identified by adding a symbol which is supposed to suggest suggest the idea of a human control point. (Think of the square as being an "unnatural," human-made shape, as opposed to the circle, which more often appears in nature.) Inside the square we place the *direction* of the control, white for positive, gray for negative, and mixed meaning the choice is still open. In the figure, we've modeled a person who responds to increased weight by *increased* exercise, and to work lost by *decreased* eating, but could decide either way about how exercise will be influenced by lost work. Notice how many more stabilizing (negative) feedback loops have been created by explicitly taking charge of your role as a controller.

For the remainder of this volume, we'll work on describing many important "laws of software engineering management." One of our most important tasks is not merely describing these laws, but in distinguishing which ones are

- "natural" laws that we'll have to learn to accept

- "human decision" laws, that we'll have to learn to control.

If you want to be the one who steers software, you'd better learn to pay attention to the difference.

## 7.4 Helpful Hints and Suggestions

- When first working with the diagram of effects, be very sure that the people understand the difference between this diagram and a process diagram such as used in describing methodologies. It may help to have them brainstorm some measures that:

a. are directly connected with one product in their process model

b. are directly connected with one stage in their process model

c. are connected with more than one stage

d. are connected with more than one product

e. cannot be connected only with stages

f. cannot be connected only with products

• People may have to practice seeing things they don't ordinarily see, but the practice will usually pay off immediately in better control. For more on how to see what you're not seeing, look at *The Secrets of Consulting.*

• People's language often reveals when they believe that they are victims of events, rather than having a choice of reactions to the event. For instance, people say things like these:

• "We <u>had to</u> ship the product on schedule."

• "The project was late, <u>so</u> we accelerated the testing."

which *sound* like they are enunciating laws of nature. Learn to listen for falsely deterministic key words such as "had to" and "so." Then politely ask, "Could you show me the reasoning behind that statement?"

## 7.5 Summary

1. Many otherwise good ideal methodologies fail to help prevent collapse because they don't prescribe negative feedback actions to be taken when the project deviates from the ideal model.

2. When the methodologies do prescribe feedback, they often speak only of the product level, or feedback steps that are too large. To be effective for control, feedback must operate in small increments, at all levels, personal, product, process, and cultural.

3. Software professionals often overlook the human decision point in models of effects. One reason is their inability to visualize certain states at all, often because they are "other outputs" of the process, and not directly connected with the product.

4. To control a project successfully, you have to learn that you need not be a victim of the dynamics. When human decision points are involved, it's not the event that counts, it's your *reaction* to the event.

## 7.6 Practice

1. Using a diagram of effects that you have developed to describe some software engineering behavior, label the diagram to show which are human decision points. Label these points to show how they are ordinarily decided in projects you have experienced.

2. Take the diagram from (1) and reverse one or more of the ordinary human decisions. Describe the change that makes in the resulting behavior.

3. Recall some dramatic event that forced you to make a quick decision. Looking back over that decision, list at least 3 alternatives you had. Describe the probable consequences of each, and compare them with the actual consequences of your decision.

4. For one day at work, carry a note pad and record every instance you hear of someone asserting a human decision law as if it were a natural law. What patterns do you see in these statements?

What do they tell you about your organization?

# Chapter 8: Failing to Steer

*"There's only one sin, and that's failing to believe you have a choice."*

- *Jean Paul Sartre*

In Chapter 4, we learned that to steer a software engineering project, the manager needs to

- plan what should happen

- observe what significant things are really happening

- compare the observed with the planned

- take actions needed to bring actual closer to planned

(Figure 8-1).

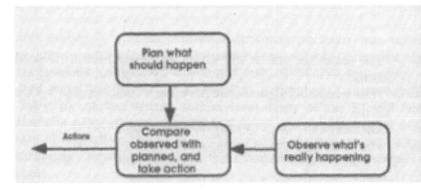

**Figure 8-1. Figure 4-5 repeated. What is necessary to steer a software engineering project.**

Pattern 2 managers are able to plan what should happen. If

they wish to move to Pattern 3, they need to learn to learn to do the other three things. In this chapter, we'll study three dynamics that commonly stand in their way. Each of these dynamics is accompanied by a "rational" explanation:

- "I'm just a victim."
- "I don't want to hear any of that negative talk."
- "I thought I was doing the right thing."

## 8.1. "I'm Just a Victim"

In 1956, I predicted that FORTRAN wouldn't last 3 years, and that was only the first of many gross mistakes I've made in my career. Let me tell you the story of how I almost made an even bigger mistake.

### 8.1.1. What distinguishes failures from successes?

In 1961, when I was at the IBM Systems Research Institute, I commissioned a student project to study software development projects that had failed. The students interviewed about a dozen project managers and derived a number of factors that had contributed to each project's failure. When we studied these factors, the only one they seemed to have in common was "bad luck." There had been floods in the computing center, flu epidemics, essential employees leaving at crucial times, blizzards, lost source files, even an earthquake. Clearly, each of these project managers had been victims of "natural laws."

The students wrote a paper documenting this astonishing but discouraging finding. I edited it, added a few thoughts of my own, and made a few calls to journal editors. One of these editors asked me whether we couldn't give the article a more positive tone by describing the factors that the successful projects had in common.

"We didn't study any successful projects," I said.

"Then how do you know they didn't also have bad luck?" (Click)

The "click" was the sound of his phone going dead and—a millisecond later—of my brain coming alive. We withdrew the paper until another group of students conducted a similar survey of successful projects. In each of these projects, too, there had been some "natural" disaster—but the results were entirely different.

Particularly striking was the contrast between two organizations that were hit by fires in the computing center. One project failed utterly, but the other recovered because it had been managed differently:

1. Backups of all source code had been stored off site, and were not affected by the fire damage. In the failed project, there were some backups, but nothing systematic.

2. Standard architectures had been used, so damaged hardware was readily replaced. In the failed project, a few thousand dollars had been saved by using "almost standard" hardware.

3. The entire staff was willing and able to pitch in and work overtime to clean up, restore files, and sort out project documentation. In the failed project, about 20% of the employees took the fire as an excuse and opportunity to leave for greener pastures.

4. Since everything had to be restructured anyway, consultants were brought in to help the project use the fire as an opportunity to reorganize. In the failed project, the only "opportunity" people saw was the chance to blame the fire for the failure they already saw was inevitable before the fire broke out.

In short, what made the difference was not the event, but their reaction to the event. The successes reacted by acknowledging a tough break, then taking charge of the recovery—even seizing the opportunity to take advantage of the "disaster." The failures, on the other hand, seized the opportunity to play victim. As the manager said, "What could I do? The whole place burned down."

### 8.1.2 Victim language

Since that time, I've never been asked to consult about a fire in the computing center, but I've certainly been called in to help many other troubled projects. In those cases, I always listen for "victim language" on the part of the managers. If I hear any, I work with these "victims" to develop diagrams of effects that clearly label points of potential human control.

A typical piece of victim language is when a manager says,

"The project is behind schedule, and I can't do anything because Brooks's Law says I can't add people without making the project fall further behind." Let's examine how to reframe this from victim language into "controller language."

Ardella was a project manager who added workers and then noticed that the project was falling behind. At that point, Ardella could continue adding workers, which would create a positive feedback loop that did not exist without management intervention, as we saw in Figure 6-4. I was called in to help, so the first thing I did was show Ardella why her own decisions are making the situation worse. This convinced her to stop adding workers, which was not exactly what I had in mind.

Figure 8-2 shows how we redrew Figure 6-4 to emphasize to Ardella that she had control in several places.

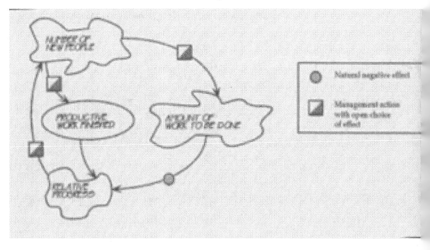

**Figure 8-2. The dynamics of Brooks's Law redrawn to suggest where a manager might look to prevent management-induced schedule delays. The difference between this figure and Figure 6-4 is the addition of human choice points.**

The human choice points suggested that there might be ways to add people without disturbing the work of the experienced people, and without increasing the coordination effort. It was Ardella's job to look for such ways, but that was the easy problem. Once she recognized that she was not a helpless victim, she took several steps to control the effect of "number of new people" on "productive work. " She set some newcomers to

- review designs and code
- update the project documentation
- create test cases
- do "gopher" work at the requests of the other workers.

Thus, although she continued to add new people (as indicated by the gray square), she made their effect positive, as shown by the white "human control" square in the diagram of Figure 8-3. While doing so, she did add some new work burden to the experienced people, though she controlled this also by giving strict instructions not to speak to the experienced workers without coming to her first. She also cut out a few work requirements that were not essential. Her partial control of the effect of "number of new people" on "amount of work to be done" is indicated in Figure 8-3 by the half-and-half symbol.

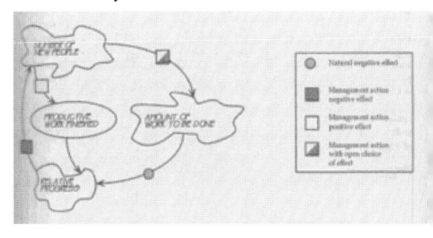

**Figure 8-3. Figure 8-2 redrawn to reflect Ardella's actual choices for managing the schedule problem.**

In short, Ardella took charge of creating her own laws, as represented by the new diagram of effects in Figure 8-3. If you, on the other hand, prefer to have the certainty of "natural" laws, I can recommend one law of human behavior that has that kind of "natural" predictability. Any time you say, "I <u>can't</u> do that," you'll always be right. The trouble is, though, that sometimes you'll also be an unnecessary victim.

### 8.2. "I Don't Want to Hear Any of That Negative Talk."

Even when managers are willing to take responsibility for their own control actions, they can't be effective unless they have accurate observations on which to choose those actions. Accurate observation doesn't happen by accident, but only by conscious

196

management decision.

Peter was a development manager who seemed to understand the software development process, but continually made inappropriate interventions to deal with a crisis of poor quality code. Our investigations of several projects under Peter's direction showed us that Peter's poor decisions were based not on poor judgment, but on misleading information about the true state of software quality.

What caused the poor quality information? When the project started to experience quality problems, fear of what would happen if the problems were accurately reported led people to take action that destroyed the accuracy of the reports, such as,

1. The test engineers would fix some problems on the spot, and not report them in the official channels.

2. The test team leader would reclassify some of the problems downward in severity.

3. The programmers would fix a group of faults and report that it was actually only a single fault that led to many failures.

4. The programming team leader would define as as many failures as possible under such categories as "customer misreading documentation" and "operating system glitch." These categories directed attention away from the programming team.

5. The project manager would "adjust" the trouble reports

with all sorts of "best case" interpretations.

These actions produced a set of highly misleading reports. No controller could have used them as the basis for an intelligent intervention. To demonstrate to Peter what we thought was going on, we sketched the positive feedback loop of Figure 8-4.

When Peter saw this diagram of effects, he responded with victim language. "Well, if that's what's going on, there's nothing I can do about it. Look, there are no human control points in the loop. People will naturally fear reporting accurately when there are lots of problems, and if they're afraid, they'll always find ways to make things look better. If the reports I get are inaccurate, there's nothing I can do to be effective, and if I'm ineffective, there will be more and more quality problems. So, by your own modeling, I'm stuck in a positive feedback loop."

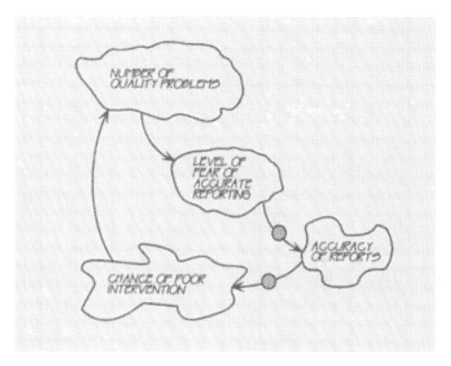

**Figure 8-4. Fear of consequences of accurate reporting of bad news leads to distorted trouble reports, making it unlikely the manager will implement meaningful interventions. This creates a positive feedback loop on poor quality.**

Peter was partially correct. If the diagram of Figure 8-4 were the total dynamic, he was indeed helpless. But a manager can always create a new diagram by adding something to the system. Together, we worked out the diagram of effects shown in Figure 8-5, which added the possibility that managers (perhaps unconsciously) could punish anyone who provided accurate measurements of quality problems. This action creates yet another feedback loop that reinforces people's natural fear of giving a poor looking report.

Though this second loop seems to make matters worse, it does have a human control point, so "worse" or "better" is subject to control. The managers do not have to punish people for providing accurate, but uncomfortable, information. If punishing messengers leads to the collapse of the information system, why not take steps to reverse this effect and reward accurate reports? Reversing this punishment effect creates a stabilizing negative feedback loop that prevents the natural fear of accurate reporting from getting totally out of hand.

I wish I could report that Peter corrected the situation immediately, but how could he? As we've seen, non-linear situations like this are not easily reversible. Trust takes years to build, but can be destroyed in a minute. Peter did inaugurate a program of management training, especially emphasizing communication skills. He set a good example by being the first to attend.

I worked with Peter's company long enough to hear him change some of his own unintended strong language, but not long enough to see whether he succeeded in undoing the Pattern 2 taboo against "negative talk." As in all cases where fear is one of the variables, prevention would have certainly been sixteen times easier than cure. People are all too ready to fear the worst from their managers, so it doesn't take a very strong dynamic to set them off.

In the following chapters, we'll see many other examples of how such unconscious or uninformed management decisions can create the positive feedback loops that lead to an unproductive situation that's difficult to reverse. More important, we'll also see how they can make conscious, informed decisions to create negative feedbacks that can eventually restore productivity—and perhaps prevent the situation next time around.

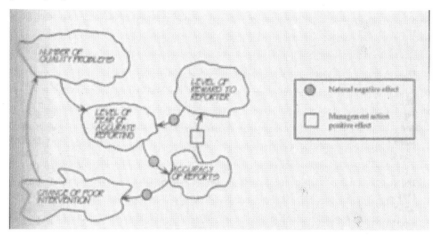

**Figure 8-5. One way a manager can react to reports of quality problems is to punish the reporter. A different approach is to reward accurate reports, which may not eliminate fear, but will help keep it under control.**

### 8.3. "I Thought I Was Doing The Right Thing."

People often act on wrong intervention models. They think they are doing "the right thing," but they're not. Worse than that, people sometimes have their intervention models backwards. They think they are doing "the right thing," but they're actually doing precisely the wrong thing. Here's a funny story in which I played the dumb victim:

Dani and I bought a dual-control electric blanket to protect our aging bones from the cruel Nebraska winter. The first night we brought it home, it didn't work, and we were both miserable. We took it back to Sears, and the salesman said he would happily take it back. First though, he asked if he could check the controls. He demonstrated that the controls were accidentally crossed, leading to the effects diagram in Figure 8-6.

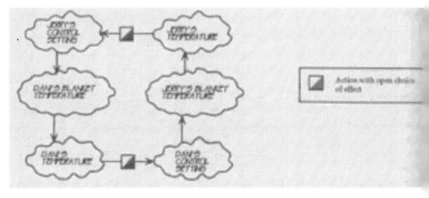

**Figure 8-6. How the dual-control blanket is cross-connected.**

This dynamic is not a victim dynamic, but relies on our conscious actions—which happened to be based on our faulty models of how the blanket really worked. My model said, "When I turn my control down, my side of the bed gets cooler." Dani's model said, "When I turn my control up, my side of the bed gets warmer." These models work well, and we would both comfortable, unless the controls are crossed. Then the dynamic is as is a runaway to the maximum discomfort the blanket can provide.

Dani and I both had backwards models of how the blanket actually worked. When she is too cold, she tries to improve the situation by turning up her control, but that results in my becoming warmer. As I am now too warm, my model dictates that I turn my control down, which actually results in Dani getting cooler. So, in the end, her action to make herself warmer actually results in a boomerang effect, and she is colder than if she had left things alone.

It was very tempting for me to blame Dani for my discomfort, but it's meaningless in such a system to ask who's controlling whom. If anything, the person who connected the controls is controlling everybody, but it might be more accurate to say that our ignorance is in control. Perhaps that's why blaming is characteristic of many Pattern 2 organizations.

Certainly the cross-connected electric blanket exactly models many situations in Pattern 2 software organizations.

United Cigar Rentals was trying hard to move to Pattern 3. For instance, they had adopted Gilb's evolutionary approach for building an order-entry system. Some internal customers were not satisfied with the quality of their micro-project. They were also unhappy because enhancements to the system were delayed to the next micro-project. They pushed the developer for speedy delivery. They also requested more functions in the next micro-project, because,

1. Recovery functions were needed primarily because of the frequent software failures.

2. They were waiting so long anyway, they wanted to get more for their patience.

The development department then let quality slip in the next micro-project in order to get all the new function delivered on time. The customer's faulty model of software development was thus "confirmed," and another cycle started with the next micro-project. (See Figure 8-7)

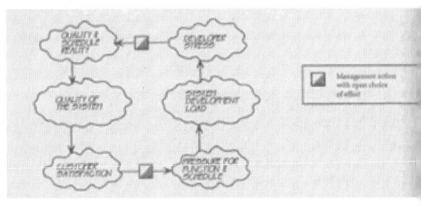

**Figure 8-7. It's possible for a software developer and customer to get cross-connected just like an electric blanket.**

UCR worked their way out of this mess by

1. teaching both parties the dynamic model shown in Figure 8-7

2. showing each that they did have control points, but they were using them backwards

3. negotiating a trust period in which the customers reduced the pressure and developers cut back on promised functions and while extending delivery times.

The success of this strategy was aided by UCR's use of the micro-project approach, because none of these actions were too large for either party to accept.

One programmer suggested to me that his managers would be doing a decent job—if only they would reverse every one of their management decisions. Unfortunately, it's not that easy. The electric blanket boomerang phenomenon was a favorite theme of Greek drama, thousands of years before there were electric blankets, or software. Oedipus' father tried to avoid his prophesied death—yet his actions led to his death. Oedipus desired to see the truth, so his actions made him blind. To avoid such boomerangs, you have to understand feedback effects, and you have to do something about them.

## 8.4 Helpful Hints and Suggestions

• Tools do not determine how they will be used. Therefore, it's not the tool that counts, it's your reaction to the tool. Programming tools can be used to program without understanding, or they can be used to free the programmer's minds and hands for tasks that can't be made routine. Pattern 2 managers buy tools

• The same distinction can be made in managing software. Management tools (such as methodologies) can be used to manage without understanding, or they can be used to free the programmer's minds and hands for tasks that can't be made routine. The first is the Pattern 2 choice; the second, Pattern 3.

• When you hear two parties blaming each other, the chances are high that they are caught in a mutually destructive feedback loop. With improved understanding of the system that has them caught, they can usually work their way out—but only if things have not gotten so far that they want revenge more than they want the original solution.

## 8.5 Summary

1. Many project managers fail to steer well because they believe they are victims, with no control over the destiny of their project. You can easily identify these managers by their use of "victim language."

2. Brooks's Law doesn't have to be a victim law if the manager recognizes where the managerial control is, and that this control can take different forms.

3. A common dynamic is punishing the messenger who brings

accurate but bad news about project progress. This intervention avoids "negative talk," but also diminishes the chance of the manager's making effective interventions needed to keep a project on the road.

4. Since the time of the Greeks, people have not only gotten their interventions wrong, they've gotten them backwards. Laying out a clear diagram of effects can help you sort out a situation in which two parties are driving each other to destruction, all the while thinking they are helping the situation.

## 8.6. Practice

1. Give three examples of victim dynamics from your own experience. Create a diagram of effects for each, and show some of the control alternatives available to the "victim." In at least one of the examples, you should have been one of the "victims."

2. Give three examples of "negative talk" situations from your own experience. How was the situation created? Was it ever corrected, and if so, by what means? How long did it take?

3. Give three examples of electric blanket dynamics from your own experience. Create a diagram of effects for each. In at least one of the examples, you should have been one of the sufferers. How did you discover that you had things backwards? How did you feel when you found out?

# Part III Demands That Stress Patterns

Organizations don't choose their patterns at random. Each pattern is a response to a series of demands placed on the organization. There are the demands of their customers, the demands of the type of problem they are trying to solve, and the internal demands generated by the way they did things in the past.

It's the interplay of these demands that determines whether an organization even has a chance to succeed using its current pattern. In the following chapters, we'll see how the external demands—customer and problem demands—stress the organization's pattern, creating the problem that its internal organization must solve. We'll also see how organizations typically respond to these demands, and what happens for each response.

# Chapter 9: Why It's Always Hard to Steer

*"Some of the cornerstones of operational management simply fall apart when used for projects. A good example is the principle of economy of scale. We all have been taught that a bigger machine using more resources at a faster rate is more efficient than a smaller counterpart; that we can achieve more economy with a process producing 5,000 nuts and bolts an hour than one producing say, ten. This law applies well in a factory*

*making nuts and bolts, but when we turn to the process of making the factory, we cannot use it. We have only one factory to be made." - Robert D. Gilbreath*

In the previous chapter, we saw several common mistakes that managers make in trying to steer software projects. Why do they make such mistakes? Are they bad people? Are they stupid people? Or are they just people, like the rest of us?

The simple fact is that if they are bad or stupid, then all of us are bad or stupid, because everyone makes such mistakes when they try to play "the game of control." In this chapter, we'll see why this game is always too hard for people to play, unless they don't care too much about how well they play.

## 9.1. The "Game of Control"

We are now in a position to understand an important distinction between two types of dynamics. We can speak of "intervention dynamics" when an essential part of the dynamic is *the human decision about how to regulate part of the process.* Brooks's Law, for example, is an intervention dynamic, because the manager could intervene differently and change the dynamic.

A "natural dynamic," on the other hand, may involve human intervention, but in a situation where there decision has no power to alter the *form* of the dynamic itself. We may "defy" the Law of Gravity by lifting things, or flying, but we have no power to change the law itself. Similarly, we can schedule programmers to work 24 hours a day, but it won't work for long, because we can't change the laws governing the physiology of sleep. In other words, natural dynamics set limits on what intervention dynamics can accomplish.

### 9.1.1 The Square Law of Computation

For those who would control software, the most important natural dynamic is the Square Law of Computation, which sets limits on what a "mind" can accomplish. To control any system, you need to be able to use your system models to compute the consequences of your planned intervention. As we've seen, these models can at least conceptually be expressed in terms of equations. Thus, every control system contains a "computer" of some sort capable of solving these equations and predicting what will happen. The computer might be a machine, but usually is a brain or a group of brains.

If a computer is to be involved, you might reasonably ask, "How big does that computer have to be?" The Square Law of Computation gives this answer:

Unless some simplification can be made,

the amount of computation to solve a set of equations

increases at least as fast as the square of the number of equations.

Since the number of equations to describe a system is equal to the number of nodes with entering arrows, or approximately the number of measurements in the system. If system A has twice the nodes of system B, then the computer for system A will need to be four times as powerful as the controller for system B.

Suppose that "computer" happens to be *you*, a software manager. Then the Square Law of Computation says that you will have to grow four times smarter at solving control problems as the system you control grows twice as big, as indicated in Figure 9-1.

Do you know how to grow four times smarter? If not, too bad, because we can see that the dynamic of Figure 9-1 is "natural." Why? Because it has no human control points, so you're not going to be able to do anything about it.

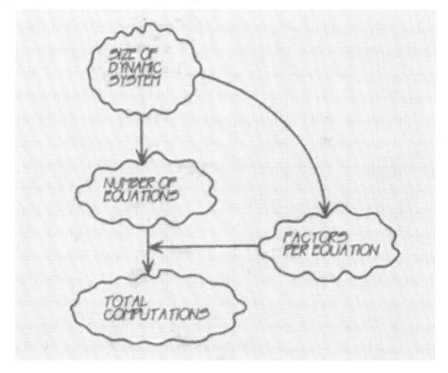

**Figure 9-1. The Square Law of Computation says that computation required to control a dynamic system grows non-linearly, which can be understood by this diagram of effects for any controller computation.**

Now, suppose that the "computer" is an entire organization cooperating to control software development. In that case, the Square Law of Computation says that the organization will have to grow 100 times more effective if it wants to build systems that are 10 times bigger! Is it any wonder that so many successful organizational patterns crumple under the stress of growth?

### 9.1.2 Control as a game

Perhaps the question should be, how is it that any software organizations manage to succeed? Games are simple examples of control situations in which we sometimes succeed in spite of their complexity. Perhaps the study of games can illuminate the question of success in the face of complexity.

How does a game model a control situation? The present position of the game is B, the initial (bad) state. Any winning position for the game is G, the good state you are trying to achieve. Your playing strategy is your way of getting from B to G, your control strategy.

Let's start with a very simple example. Tic-Tac-Toe is a *deterministic* game, so there are no random elements to contend with—except for your opponent's moves. In terms of the cybernetic model, this means there is no "randomness" input to contend with. Therefore, if your model of the game is better than mine, I can never beat you at Tic-Tac-Toe. Your model tells you how to counter every move of mine with one that's at least as good. You can look ahead and see all possible consequences of each of your possible "interventions." Thus, you are exactly in the position of the perfect controller.

In Figure 9-2, we see such a perfect controller's strategy starting from one position that might be obtained after four moves, two by X and two by O. As the complete "game tree" shows, this perfect controller can win every time from this position.

Tic-Tac-Toe, of course, does not provide a very complex regulatory situation, so your brain does not have to be very big to play a perfect game. At the Nebraska State Fair, you can pay a quarter and play Tic-Tac-Toe with trained *chickens*. The chickens *never lose*. Therefore, we can conclude that the complexity of Tic-Tac-Toe is less than the capacity of a chicken brain. No wonder we're not too impressed by Tic-Tac-Toe.

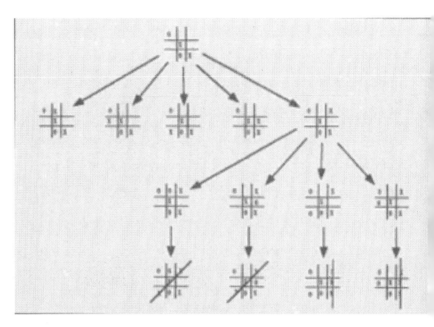

**Figure 9-2. Tic-Tac-Toe is a *deterministic* game, which means that in theory a player can look ahead and examine all possible moves, all the way to the end, to see which lead to a victory, loss, or draw. Here we see part of a game tree showing how X can achieve victory from one possible four-move position, regardless of what O plays.**

### 9.1.3 How complex is chess?

But what happens as the game gets more complex? Chess is obviously a more complex game than Tic-Tac-Toe, but it is also deterministic, because random changes in the board are not allowed. In some sense, that means chess is exactly the same game as Tic-Tac-Toe—but one that requires a bigger computer.

In other words, your chess computer can think ahead through the "game tree" just as you can in Tic-Tac-Toe. So far, however, nobody has taught a chicken how to play perfect chess, so perhaps it requires a computer bigger than a chicken brain. Neither has anybody yet taught a mechanical computer to play perfect chess, though there are many excellent chess playing programs that use this look-ahead strategy. Figure 9-3, for instance, shows a position from which the chess program "Deep Thought" found a "forced mate" (a move tree in which every branch leads to victory) in 3.5 seconds.

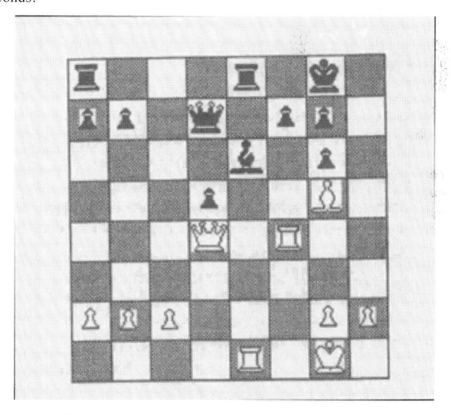

**Figure 9-3. Chess is also a deterministic game, which means that in some sense it is exactly equivalent to Tic-Tac-Toe,**

though it requires a larger computer. However, nobody has yet taught a chicken to play winning chess, though the computer program "Deep Thought" found a forced mate for White from this position in 3.5 seconds. Can you do better?

### 9.1.4 Computational complexity

The additional complexity of chess over Tic-Tac-Toe is *computational* complexity, which arises because of combinatorics. In the Tic-Tac-Toe position of Figure 9-2, there are only 5 possible moves for X, each of which is followed by 4 possible moves for O. Each of these is followed by 3 possible moves for X, each of which has two possible moves by O (although the game may be lost by then, which somewhat reduces the complexity). Thus, to examine all possible moves from this position requires consideration of 5 x 4 x 3 x 2, or 120 positions, at most. Indeed, for all possible games of Tic-Tac-Toe there are at most 9 x 8 x 7 x 6 x 5 x 4 x 3 x 2 = 362,880 sequences, which is one way to measure complexity.

Now consider the complexity of chess. From the chess position in Figure 9-3, White has 52 possible moves, each of which can be followed by a variable number of moves by Black. For instance, if White moves the king's pawn, Black has 28 possible responses. If this is the average number of responses, then there are 52 x 28 = 1456 possible White-Black combinations. Thus, even a pair of White-Black sequences have over a million combinations, which is already far more complex than Tic-Tac-Toe. Unlike Tic-Tac-Toe, a chess game is not guaranteed to end after a fixed number of moves, but if we estimate an average game has 30 move pairs, and each move pair has 1,000 combinations, then we would estimate $1,000^{30}$, or $10^{90}$ different games.

### 9.1.5 Simplification by general principles

We know that no human being has ever learned how to play perfect chess—otherwise there would have been an undefeated chess champion. *Perfect* chess is probably beyond the human computing capacity, yet many people do manage to play chess reasonably well. Because *perfect* chess is beyond their computational capacity, human beings cannot play by examining all possible moves in the game tree—except in special situations like the end game, or a forced mate.

Instead of trying to examine all possible moves, people increase their *apparent* computational capacity by applying "general principles." Examples of general chess principles are "Castle early" and "Avoid doubling pawns on the same file." Although there are exceptions to each general principle, they help reduce computational complexity by restricting examination to the "most promising" moves. This is what the Square Law of Computation means by *"Unless some simplification can be made..."*

For instance, one general principle of chess is "don't give up your queen to capture a less powerful piece." This is an excellent principle which almost always leads to superior play because you don't have to consider such queen sacrifices. In the position of Figure 9-2, however, it is exactly such a "forbidden" move that leads to a forced mate for White.

Of course, White could probably win with a number of less powerful moves, but the point is clear. "General principles" of play allow us to play better with limited computational capacity *most of the time*, but the price is that we will miss the best play *some of the time*. This is the Square Law of Computation at work, forcing us to do the best we can with our rather limited resources—limited, that is, relative to the problem we are trying to solve.

### 9.1.6 The Size/Complexity Dynamic

Now, what has this to do with software engineering? In the first place, I contend that developing perfect software is *much* harder than playing perfect chess, which is already well beyond human capacity. To deal with this complexity, The Square Law of Computation dictates that we have simplifying general principles.

If we are to have a fighting chance to produce *good* software, not to speak of *perfect* software, we *need* simplifications . These simplifications are what we call "Software Engineering." They include methodologies and effects models, implicit and explicit. They also include such "general principles" as

• "Don't add workers late in a project in an attempt to catch up."

- "Never use GO TO statements in your code."
- "Always buy the best possible tools."
- "Don't write monolithic code; break it into modules."
- "Use the smallest possible team of the best possible people."
- "Never write any code until all the design work has been reviewed."
- "Don't punish the bearer of bad news."

Integrated collections of such methods, models, and principles are what we have been calling cultural patterns. Each cultural pattern contains its own large set of simplifications for playing the game of software engineering. Like the principle, "Never sacrifice your queen," they are merely approximations that we need because of the dynamic:

*Human brain capacity is more or less fixed,*
*but software complexity grows at least as fast*
*as the square of the size of the program.*

This is probably the most important, *natural software dynamic*. It combines the Square Law of Computation with the assumption that we cannot alter our brain capacity, at least in the short run. I call it the *Size/Complexity Dynamic*.

9.2 The Size/Complexity Dynamic in Software Engineering

The Size/Complexity Dynamic important because it appears everywhere in software engineering, though often in disguise.

### 9.2.1 The history of software

Perhaps the most important place it occurs is in the entire history of the software business, which could be summarized in the diagram of effects of Figure 9-4. This diagram shows that whenever the software development business has succeeded, we have raised our ambition. Thus, the problems we attempt to solve grow bigger until they become limited by the complexity of their solution, because of the Size/Complexity Dynamic.

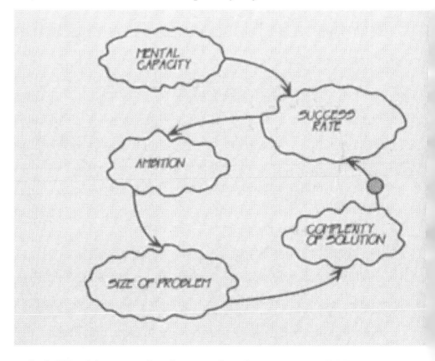

**Figure 9-4. The history of software development could be summarized in this diagram of effects, which shows how whenever we succeed, we raise our ambition. Thus, the problems we attempt to solve grow bigger until they become**

**limited by the complexity of their solution, because of the Size/ Complexity Dynamic.**

As we try to solve "bigger" problems, the Size/Complexity Dynamic drives us from a previously successful pattern to a new, untried pattern. Were it not for our insatiable ambition, we could rest comfortably with our present pattern until they carried us away in rocking chairs. Many organizations have done just that, usually because their customers have no further ambitions for "better" software.

### 9.2.2 The history of software engineering

Figure 9-4 shows that when there *is* ambition for more value in software, it quickly pushes against the barrier of the Size/ Complexity Dynamic, unless we can alter the capacity of our brains. Organizations sometimes do this by hiring smarter people, but there's a definite limit to that tactic. Several of the software organizations I work with have started complaining that there are not enough top computer science graduates to go around, which has started a bidding war for brains.

We can't alter the *capacity* of our brains, but we can alter how much of that capacity we use, and what we use it for. That's why software engineering was invented. Figure 9-5 shows how software engineering attempts to simplify the solutions to larger problems, thus raising the success rate in response to increased ambition. It also shows, if we examine its dynamics, that as long as our ambition is stimulated by success, we'll never finish the job of developing software engineering.

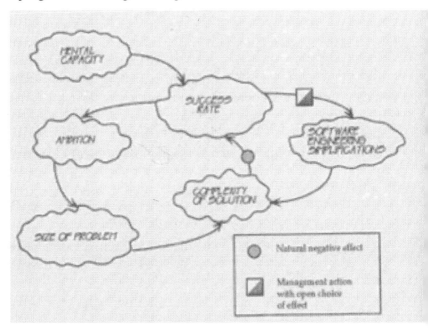

**Figure 9-5. The history of software *engineering* is the history of attempts to beat the Size/Complexity Dynamic by creating simplifications that reduce the complexity of solutions as problems grow bigger. Without ambition, there is no need for software engineering.**

Conversely, Figure 9-5 also shows that once an organization reaches the maximum level of ambition for software, there is no urge to adopt further software engineering practices, and the organization settles down into a comfortable cultural pattern. It's only when an organization reaches Pattern 4 that the ambition for higher quality becomes internalized, at which point the cycle of improved software engineering becomes self-sustaining.

### 9.2.3. Games against Nature

Each Size/Complexity Dynamic has two parts: the fixed human brain and the complexity that grows with size. Each example of the complexity a particular instance of the Square Law of Computation. For instance, we always see the Size/Complexity Dynamic in any form of game, though the particular details will vary from game to game.

A game in this general sense is a situation in which there are two players (one of whom may be "Nature", who dishes up natural dynamics that we have to beat if we are to get from B to G). The two players more or less alternate moves, and because you must respond to your opponent's move, you get a two-move dynamic shown in Figure 9-6.

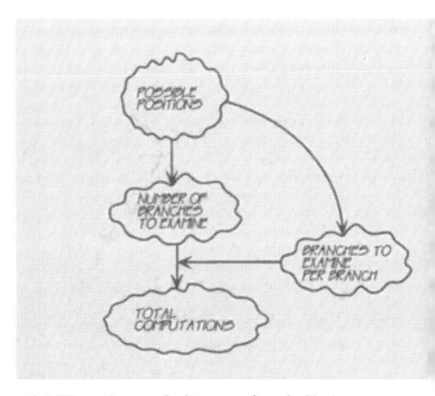

**Figure 9-6 Where the complexity comes from in Size/ Complexity Dynamic applied to playing games. By making a bigger board, you can soon make the game too complex for any player.**

This diagram could also be used to describe "the game of management," or "the game of control." It matters not whether the "opponent" is Nature (randomness) or the highly structured efforts of the other people in the organization. As controller, the manager has to respond to all moves that might start the project on a losing path. Good managers, like good poker players, don't believe in bad luck. They play well with whatever hand they're dealt.

### 9.2.4. The Fault Location Dynamic

Figure 9-7 shows one of the most important ways that the Size/Complexity Dynamic applies to the building of large systems, software or otherwise. This is the Fault Location Dynamic. It shows why more and more labor is spent locating faults as your systems get more ambitious. You'll notice that nowhere in this model is there a measure of "luck." Good programmers don't believe in luck, either.

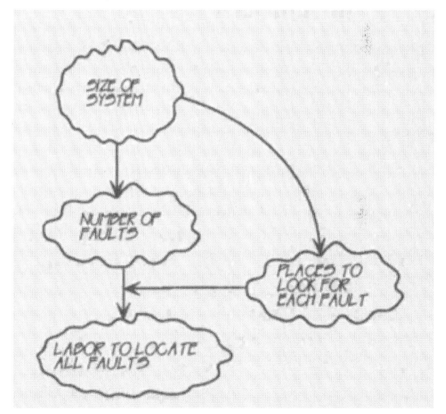

**Figure 9-7 The source of complexity in the Size/Complexity Dynamic applied to the problem of finding faults in a system. If**

225

**your development process creates faults at the same rate, your larger system will contain more faults. Since the system is bigger, there are more places to look for each fault. Thus, total fault location labor grows non-linearly. This is called the Fault Location Dynamic.**

When Pattern 2 managers start to feel the barrier created by the Fault Location Dynamic, they may not understand that this is a natural dynamic. Instead, they feel that it arises from some correctable inadequacy in the developers, like lack of attention or motivation. They don't understand that the Fault Location Dynamic describes finding faults in the *system*, not the management practice of finding faults with the *people* who are building the system and working against the troubles caused by the Fault Location Dynamic.

### 9.2.5. The Human Interaction Dynamic

In order to beat the Fault Location Dynamic (or other forms of the Size/Complexity Dynamic), Pattern 2 managers often acquire large staffs. When they do this, however, the encounter the dynamic in another of its common disguises, the Human Interaction Dynamic. The effects of this dynamic are well-known to social psychologists and project managers, who long ago observed that as you got more people, the ways they could interact tended to multiply faster than you could control them. The Human Interaction Dynamic—which we shall revisit many times—is shown in Figure 9-8.

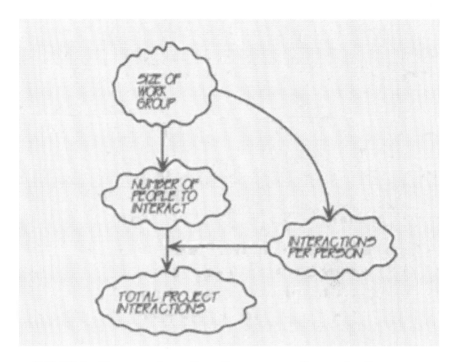

**Figure 9-8.** This diagram describes the source of complexity when the Size/Complexity Dynamic is applied to the problem of coordinating a work group (which is part of the original Brooks's Law dynamic, as well as many others). The total number of interactions grows non-linearly with the number of people in a group, so that trying to work with bigger groups adds to the internal control workload. We call this the Human Interaction Dynamic.

## 9.3 Helpful Hints and Suggestions

• Don't take the word "square" in the Square Law of Computation too seriously. There are a number of reasons why the worst power could be less non-linear. For instance,

1. The task (such as building software) is never totally mental. There are always a number of things to accomplish that have nothing to do with the size of the mental task, such as the startup overhead for any project.

2. Projects are seldom working so far out on the curve that the non-linear effects are being felt very strongly. Those that are, are probably failing, and may not make it into the statistics.

3. Our best software engineering efforts are directed at reducing the non-linearity. Modularization is one of the strongest strategies for keeping the Square Law under control. This strategy fights complexity at the large project end, but adds work at the small project end, this reducing the overall non-linearity of the size/effort curve.

• Also don't forget that it's possible to do much *worse* than the Size/Complexity Dynamic suggests. Whenever we create an intervention dynamic that contains positive feedback, we are in danger of making the size/complexity relationship not just non-linear, but exponentially non-linear. The Size/Complexity Dynamic speaks only of a limitation on good managers. Bad managers are unlimited in their potential to do mischief.

• There are many arguments that demonstrate that perfect control of software development is much harder than playing chess, but I'll give only one. On a typical computer, each machine instruction is represented by a pattern of 32 bits. Thus, one instruction can be written in $2^{32}$, or approximately $10^{10}$ ways. A sequence of two instructions can thus be written in $10^{20}$ ways, and a program only 100 lines long can be written in $10^{1000}$ ways (1 followed by 1000 zeros).

For the program to be *perfect*, we must write the sequence of instructions exactly. Writing perfect programs of even 100 lines is thus far more complex than playing perfect chess. And remember that a more typical size for a piece of commercial software might be 100,000 lines, with some running over 10,000,000.

• Do perfect programs have only one way to write them? It depends on the requirements. In chess, there are often two forced mates from the same position, taking the same number of moves, so is one of them more perfect than the other? Perhaps winning every games would be "perfect" for most chess players. Perhaps winning every tournament. Or winning only one tournament, the world title. What these arguments show is that the more flexible we are in defining "perfect," the easier the job of control. In other words, if you're willing to give up some control at the outset, you increase your chances of staying in control at the end.

## 9.4 Summary

1. Human intervention dynamics are those over which we potentially have control, but there is always a set of "natural"

dynamics which put a limit on how good a job any controller can do. A large part of the controller's job is devising intervention dynamics that can keep the natural dynamics under the best control possible, which can never be perfect.

2. The Square Law of Computation says that computational complexity grows non-linearly as the number of factors in the computation grows.

3. Control can be thought of as a game that the controller plays against "Nature." Even games of "perfect information," such as Tic-Tac-Toe and Chess, require non-linear increases in brainpower to play perfectly as the size of the "board" increases.

4. Simplification is always needed, because controllers are always playing a "game" well outside their mental capacity. Simplification takes the form of rough dynamic models and approximate rules such as "Always break a project down into modules."

5. Software engineering management is harder than Chess, because controlling a project is a game of "imperfect information," and the size of the "board" is not fixed.

6. The Size/Complexity Dynamic appears in many forms throughout software engineering, forms such as the Fault Location Dynamic and the Group Interaction Dynamic.

## 9.5 Practice

1. Tom DeMarco agrees that managing software development is harder than playing chess, but he says that my "proof" is wrong. He didn't, however, give his own proof. Give your own "proof," by which I mean an argument that convinces you. Or, if you're not convinced, give a proof of the converse.

2. Create a diagram of effects describing the " bidding war for brains" that sometimes goes on among organizations that try to push against the barrier of the Size/Complexity Dynamic by hiring more smart people. Show why, as one wag put it, "The growth of the software business has led to a flow of students from physics to computer science, with has resulted in an increase in the average intelligence of both fields." Do you believe it?

3. The idea of a "game" can be generalized to more than two players. Discuss ways in which the arguments about control of software development can be generalized to a 3-player game. Can you generalize to an N-player game?

## Chapter 10: What It Takes To Be Helpful

*"When you see someone coming to help you, run for the hills." - Thoreau*

For those of us who continue to be ambitious about software, the Size/Complexity Dynamic says we're going to need a lot of help. In this chapter, we'll look at some of the characteristics of ideas and practices that will prove helpful for staying in control of software.

## 10.1 Reasoning Graphically about the Size/Complexity Dynamic

We know that models are helpful, but different people react to the same model in different ways. That's why it's always helpful is to have different ways of representing the same ideas.

### 10.1.1. Size vs. brainpower

Figure 10-1 shows the Size/Complexity Dynamic graphically in a form that often helps thinking about it. The curved line shows that the computational power needed to control grows non-linearly with problem size. Each horizontal line represents an individual person's or organization's "brainpower." Once the control curve rises above the brainpower line, that person can no longer play a "perfect game" of controlling in that problem situation.

Figure 10-1 is an antidote to people who become overly impressed with their own IQ. Notice how one person can be twice as smart as another (whatever that means), but not be able to solve twice as big a problem. As somebody once said, "IQ scores would be a lot more meaningful if you added 10,000 to each score."

Because the Size/Complexity Dynamic is a *natural* dynamic, the kinds of improvements we can make to our computational power—our thinking—cannot ultimately grow faster than the size of the programs we attempt to write. We might paraphrase this dynamic as,

*Ambitious requirements can easily outstrip*
*even the brightest developer's mental capacity.*

Let's return to chess to see why this is so. Suppose your "customer" gave you the requirement , "Write a perfect chess playing program." And suppose you were smart enough to do it. All you would have to do to outstrip your machine's capacity is to define a new version of chess played on a larger board. A 25% increase to a 10 by 10 board will mean at least a 56% increase in the complexity of each move. And, if that isn't enough, all you would just have to increase the board to 20 by 20, or 100 by 100, until the machine—and your program—was outclassed.

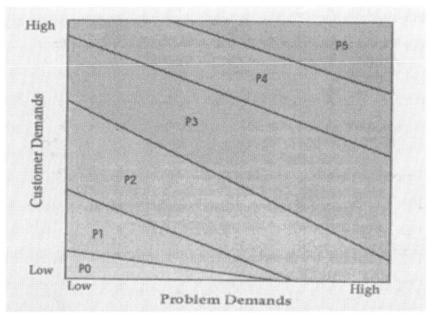

**Figure 10-1. As the size of a system grows, the complexity required to control it grows non-linearly (curved line). Any particular human brain, however, has a relatively fixed capacity, which can be represented by a horizontal line. Once the complexity curve crosses that line, the system is too complex for that brain to control perfectly.**

*10.1.2 The size vs. effort curve*

Figure 10-2 relates this type of curve in Figure 10-1 to software engineering. A particular pattern for controlling software development can be conceptually represented by a single size/effort curve, where the effort is largely mental effort. Other patterns will be represented by other size/effort curves. Each curve shows how well its pattern *can* do on problems of different size. It doesn't show how well its pattern *will* do, because incompetent

234

managers can always make a project go worse than it could have gone.

Each size/effort curve can be used as an estimating tool for a particular pattern.

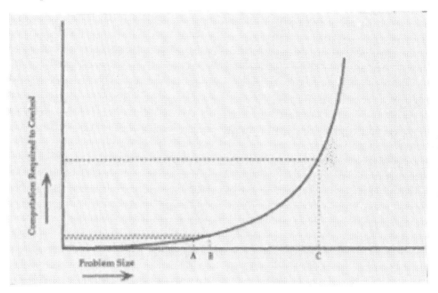

**Figure 10-2. A particular software engineering method can be represented as a curve relating size and complexity. Points A, B, and C represent three different size requirements, with B representing a 10 per cent increase over A, and C representing a 100 per cent increase. Using this method, the complexity of solving B is only about 10 per cent greater than A, but C is about 1300 per cent greater.**

Let's see how to use this curve in estimating. Suppose you were doing a project of size A, and were asked to increase the problem size by adding a few requirements. This would bring the project to size B, which you estimated to be about a 10% increase in requirements. According to the estimating curve, developing B using the same cultural pattern would require about 10% more work. In other words, the curve for this pattern is still relatively linear at point B.

But suppose you are asked to add requirements to bring the problem to point C, about doubling the size at A. For a problem of this size, the curve estimating your pattern is quite non-linear. The curve shows that the workload will ascend much faster than you would have estimated—had you extrapolated linearly. As estimated on this curve, the workload at C is about 13 times that at A, although the system is only twice as "big" by one method of measuring, such as lines of code or function points.

### 10.1.3 Variation and the Log-Log Law

The Size/Complexity Dynamic is universal and has been known for almost the entire history of software. So why do project managers continue to dupe themselves with linear estimation fallacies? Some of them, of course, never study history, and so are condemned to relive it. But others are misled by two factors, variation and the Log-Log Law.

One of my clients, whom we'll call the "Canadian American Border Fence Company" (CABFC), decided to use a size/effort curve for estimating projects. Figure 10-3 shows their data from a dozen past projects. Their plot was typical of plots that have been presented in the literature for decades, so I thought they would

impress Alger McKewan, CABFC's Manager of Information
Systems. When I showed him the plot to demonstrate the Size/
Complexity Dynamic, he gave me a blank look. I used his Mac to
draw in the curved line shown, which was a best statistical fit.
Instead of being convinced, he pushed me aside, punched a few
keys, and produced the straight line—*another* best statistical fit.

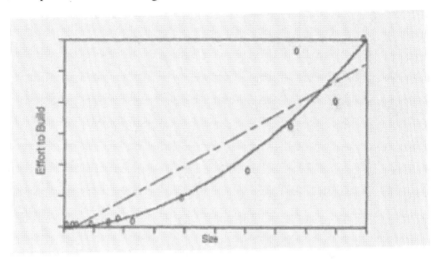

**Figure 10-3. Among all the variation in real data, it may be
hard to distinguish the non-linear nature of the size/effort
relationship.**

What had gone wrong with my convincing argument?
Mathematically, the residuals were smaller with my curve (i.e, it
was a "better" fit), but that would be expected because my curve
used one more parameter than his linear fit. The trouble was, of
course, the *variability* in software productivity data, which has
been well know for decades. The Size/Complexity Dynamic is

only a *tendency*—albeit a strong one—and just one of many factors that may influence the amount of work that goes into a particular project. Thus, any one organization may have difficulty visualizing the idealized dynamic within the real data, even if they keep data on a fairly large number of projects.

Paradoxically, the other factor that obscures the Size/Complexity Dynamic arises from the attempt to make such variable data more convincing. For some years, now, almost all of the public presentations of size versus effort data seem to be plotted on log-log scales, such as Figure 10-4, which re-plots CABFC's data of Figure 10-3. You will notice how well this log-log straight line seems to fit the data. That's not surprising, because the Log-Log Law says,

*Any set of data points forms a straight line if plotted on log-log paper.*

Of course, the Log-Log Law is not strictly true, but is a fairly strong observation about the way the human eye senses data. By using a log-log plot, researches can impress you that their data have "meaning." In the process, however, they may obscure the most important meaning—that the relationship between size and effort is non-linear. This log-log practice is especially misleading for project managers, who are too busy fighting the practical consequences of the Size/Complexity Dynamic to read software engineering articles very carefully.

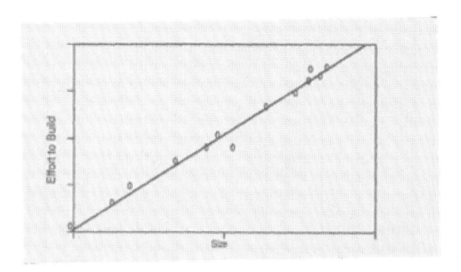

**Figure 10-4. The tendency to plot experimental data on a log log scale tends to further obscure the non-linear nature of the size/effort relationship—especially to busy project managers reading articles by glancing at the pictures.**

## 10.2. Comparing Patterns and Technologies

One of the most important ways a manager tries to be helpful is by choosing technologies that will be part of the organization's cultural pattern—and ultimately choosing the entire pattern. Such choices can never be exact, but they are well suited for graphic reasoning.

### 10.2.1. Comparing with a size/effort curve

Since a size/effort curve can be used to characterize a software engineering pattern, two different patterns can be compared by showing curves for the two approaches to solving the same set of problems. Figure 10-5 shows two general curves demonstrating how this is done.

Methods 1 and 2 could represent entire patterns, such as Variable (1) and Routine(2). They could also represent parts of patterns, such as,

- two programmers of different skill
- a programmer versus a programming team
- one organization's entire programming staff versus another's
- two different programming tools or languages
- one organization before and after adopting new practices.

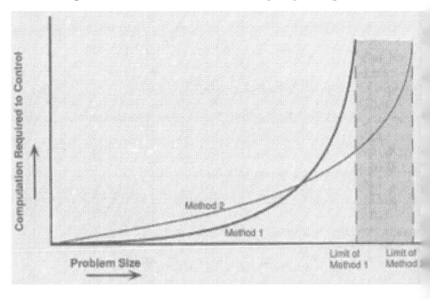

**Figure 10-5. The two software engineering methods can be compared by comparing their size/computation curves. Method 1 costs less for working with small systems, but reaches a limit first. Method 2 can control systems larger than**

**anything Method 1 can control (in the shaded region) but because of the Size/Complexity Dynamic also eventually reaches an effective limit.**

Regardless of what they specifically represent, we notice in the figure how Method 1 is better for small problems, but runs out of computational capacity before Method 2. Method 2 could be thought of as the "smarter" method, because it can control more complex systems. But, no matter how much smarter one programmer is, or what excellent practices are adopted, Method 2's curve has the same *natural* dynamic — the Size/Complexity Dynamic. Therefore, though Method 2 can push the complexity limit further to the right, it must always reach some limit of the system it can control.

### *10.2.2 Seeing through the data*

Figure 10-6 shows a size/effort plot of some data taken from experiments with the Focus and COBOL programming languages, which could be our Method 1 and Method 2. As usual, it's a bit hard to see exactly which method is better among the scatter of data points, but Figure 10-7 shows the best linear fit to the two methods.

Looking at these two straight lines, we could easily be convinced that "Focus is better than COBOL." Indeed, many software managers have come to such a conclusion about "fourth generation languages." But the data of Figure 10-7 were taken from relatively small-scale, though well controlled, experiments. In actual practice, when larger programs are attempted, the curves for Focus and COBOL probably look like Figure 10-5. At a certain point, the expressive and computational power of the fourth generation language runs out of steam, and the clumsier third generation language can still be pushed a bit further.

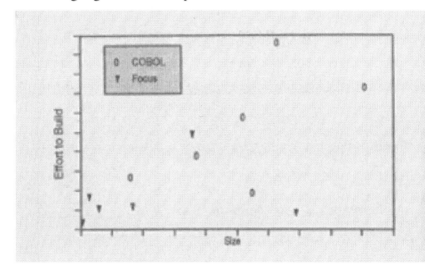

**Figure 10-6. Among all the variation in real data, it may also be hard to distinguish two different methods in a small set of experiments.**

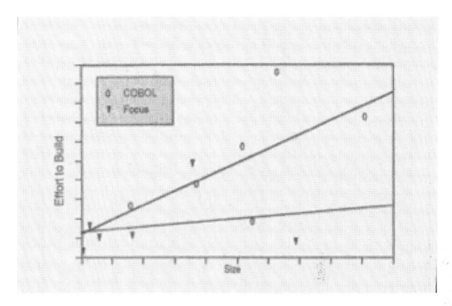

**Figure 10-7.** The best fit lines help us to distinguish the two sets of data, but may fool us into thinking this is a linear relationship, rather than the early part of a non-linear curve such as Figure 10-7.

### 10.2.3. Combining two methods into a composite pattern

Because two methods may excel on problems of different magnitudes, we often find organizations using two or more methods for software development. A Steering manager is not afraid to have a toolkit of methods, even though that adds the additional task of choosing which method to use when.

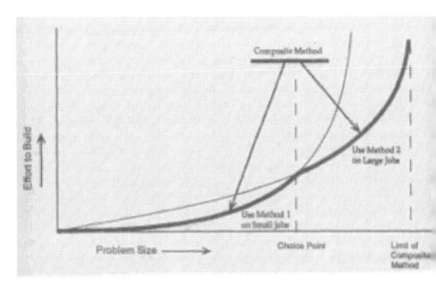

**Figure 10-8. When two methods differ greatly in their ability to handle different size problems, an organization may choose to use both, one for small problems and the other for large problems. This composite method consists of the two original methods plus a method for making the choice between them.**

In the situation of Figure 10-5, Method 1 would be used for small jobs and Method 2 used for large jobs, yielding the composite method shown in Figure 10-8. At least, that's the ideal. In many Routine organizations, Method 1 is used by those programmers and managers who *know* Method 1, and Method 2 by programmers and managers who *know* Method 2.

Employing a composite method, burdens managers with an extra decision on each job. What is the choice point for choosing one method over another? Routine managers living in a blaming environment would prefer not to have this choice. That way, when

244

the project fails, they can plead, "Well, we followed the standard method all the way, so it's not my fault."

### 10.2.4. Choosing for reasons other than effort

This example suggests that managers choose methods for reasons other than the total effort they will require. Perhaps the most frequent reason, other than effort, is *risk*. Figure 10-9 shows a size/risk graph that can be used as an aid in this decision situation.

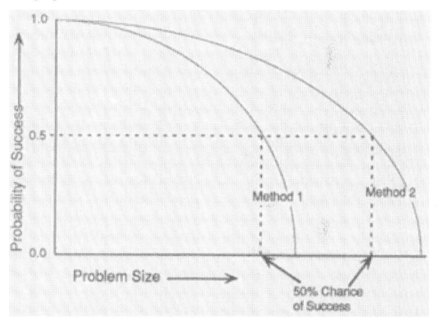

**Figure 10-9. A size/risk graph, showing how a project's chance of success depends on its size, for each of two methods. At the size where Method 1 has a 50 per cent chance of success, Method 2 has about an 80 per cent chance of success. Method 2 is obviously safer, though it says nothing about how much this safety will cost. For that, we'd need a size/effort graph.**

A graph of this form highlights the maxim that "money can't

buy everything," for each curve represents the best chance you have with its method, no matter how much you're willing to spend. At the size where Method 1 has a 50% chance of success, Method 2 has about an 80% chance of success. Method 2 is obviously safer, if we're willing to pay the price, though the graph says nothing about what this price will be. For that, we'd need a size/effort graph to use in conjunction with the size/risk graph.

Figure 10-10 suggests another interpretation of Figure 10-9. Human beings take time to learn, so whenever we use a new method, the first time costs more and is more risky. Figure 10-10 is a size/risk graph in which the two curves represent the first and second times we attempt to use a new method—which could be a new programming language, a new project management system, or even a new pattern.

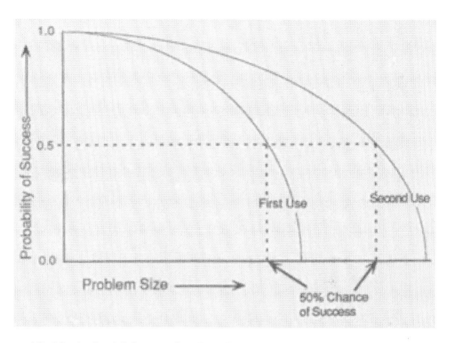

**Figure 10-10. A size/risk graph, showing how a project's chance of success depends on its size, the first and second times a new method is used.**

### 10.2.5. Reducing the risk of change

This size/risk graph captures the idea, in terms of risk, that the first time is always harder. Managers studying this graph might decide that their career progress cannot afford this level of risk, so they'll let someone else be first. The decision to "always be second" almost always makes sense to the individual manager. Thus, in order to move from one method to another, the risk on the decision maker has to be reduced. There are several tactics to help this change happen:

1. *Move the decision to higher level of management.* For a

higher level manager, this will be only one risk of many, so the risk is spread. It may, however, be difficult to find a lower level manager willing to accept this project.

2. *Reduce the size of the first project.* This is the concept behind the *pilot project.* Unfortunately, many pilots forget this concept and choose a big project in order "to attract attention for the new technology." This is a poor strategy, because the first time has a high risk of failure. If it's attention you want, get it on a project that succeeds, rather than one that fails. To do that, dedicate the first pilot to *learning*, and the second to attention-getting. The first pilot can then only fail if you fail to learn from it.

3. *Reduce the criticality of the first project.* This is another concept behind the *pilot project.* It's fine to say that you're dedicating the first pilot to learning, but that won't work if the users are depending on the first pilot to make millions. If you fail, you may not be given the opportunity to apply your learning to the next project.

Tactics such as these will help raise the chance of successful technology transfer, but nothing can guarantee success with a new technology, no matter how helpful it promises to be. The use of graphical reasoning will, however, guarantee that you don't fail because you failed to consider some important tradeoff. That's all you can ask from a management tool.

## 10.3 Helpful Interactions

Now we can better understand the questions:

*"How is it we keep doing harmful things over and over, even when we know better?"*

*"How can we be more helpful, more consistently?"*

### 10.3.1. Do no harm.

We do harmful things because we're trying to control systems that are beyond our mental capacity to control perfectly. That means:

1. We may not really know better, because what we "know" may only be a simplification like "never sacrifice your queen" that we've carried over from simpler control situations.

2. We may not be able to see the true dynamics because so many dynamics combine to produce data with a high degree of variation. Only after we bring one dynamic after another under our control will this "randomness" start to disappear, and our process become easier to understand. This kind of stability is what you need to move from Pattern 2 to Pattern 3.

3. With all these confusions, the short-term effects of the behavior may, but the long-term effects are harmful, and we are not smart enough to see the connection. This kind of dynamic can create an *addiction*, which need not be to drugs. We can be addicted to any behaviors, such as patching code directly in machine language. All such addictions are ultimately based on

faulty intervention models—diseases of limited intelligence.

### 10.3.2 The Helpful Model

We are always trying to make sense of our world, to control it as much as we can, but the world is naturally more complex than our brains. We have simplifying models to help us measure what's going on and determine what to do about it. Because our models are only approximations, there are many ways we can fail. Or you can fail when I don't.

Sometimes, though, you are not failing at all. It's just that your models are not necessarily the same as mine, and that, in fact, our models may be exact opposites. So, when I see you doing something that seems to be making the situation worse, I don't immediately assume that you are *trying* to do harm. Instead, I apply what I call *The Helpful Model*:

*No matter how it looks,*
*everyone is trying to be helpful.*

I often see interventions so bizarre that I get the impression people are attempting to sabotage the project and make me miserable. My "Helpful Model" leads me to see where other people's models of "being helpful" are going wrong, and to deal more rationally with my own feelings of paranoia.

Even when people's models are the same, they may be pursing different *objectives*. Using trade-off graphs such as size/effort and size/risk will help make these objectives available for public discussion—but why would someone want to discuss trade-offs with someone they feel is trying to sabotage their efforts? If you're trying to save money while I'm secretly trembling with fear of project failure, my contributions are not likely to seem helpful to you, so always start by calling upon the Helpful Model.

The Helpful Model works for me because it takes away blame and lets me look at the dynamics, independent of anybody's intention. It also explains why you would persist in doing something that wasn't helpful. Believing your intervention is helpful, you will persist with enough strength to create a new intervention dynamic. Nobody has that much energy or patience for sabotage.

### 10.3.3 The Principle of Addition

To get rid of dysfunctional intervention dynamics, people's models must be changed. In a computer, you can simply erase the memory and load a new program, but people's brains don't work that way. Everything you have ever known is stored somewhere in your brain, so you can never eliminate mental models; you can only *add* to them. That's why this book is based on *The Principle of Addition*:

*The best way to reduce ineffective behavior*
*is by adding a more effective behavior.*

And that's ultimately the way we help an organization move from one pattern to another. As they add more effective models, they find them used more and more, and this simply leaves less opportunity for the ineffective ones to be used. Here's an example:

Organizations get addicted to certain practices because although those practice are harmful in the long run, they relieve their pain in the short run. The more they do them, the worse they feel—and the more they seek the relief of their addictive practices.

To counter a practice to which an organization is addicted, you can add a long-range component to their model. You need to measure in the long range, and reward and punish in the long range. Thus, if you find an organization that is addicted to some short-sighted intervention, you have to look for what rewards (explicit or implicit) are given for short-run success in this behavior. You remove those if you can, and you supplement them with rewards that are tied to long-run success.

We cured one organization of code patching by a combination of interventions.

1. Patching was rewarding because the procedure seemed so much simpler than using the official configuration management system. We providing a better configuration tool, to make patching only marginally simpler than using the standard procedure.

2. Programmers were often rewarded for getting a product shipped on time, even if they did it through bypassing the build procedures. Rather than trying to subtract this reward, we taught the managers to give even greater praise to programmers who

conformed to build standards and still shipped on time.

### *10.3.4. Adding to the repertoire of models*

By such a process of adding new systems of reinforcement, you may extinguish an addictive behavior. By adding a different model, however, you could do even better—you might prevent the addiction in the first place. That's because of the strong role that models play in people's behavior:

*The way people behave is not based on reality,*
*but on their **models** of reality.*

Here's an example:

I was working with a manager on the case of a "problem employee." I was trying to get him to see that he was placating the employee, and by not confronting him, he was creating a co-dependent situation. I got nowhere, and finally told the manager that I was going to stop, as I couldn't help him on this problem. The manager agreed.

As we were walking out of the room, the manager asked, "Now that that's done, can you help me with a personal problem?" We went back into the room to work on his "personal problem." He was a new manager who felt he was losing his technical abilities, and he lacked confidence. Once we got somewhere with his confidence, he stopped seeing the "problem employee" as a problem. The manager did what I suggested he do in the first place, but under a different model of what he was doing.

People with appropriate, effective models will never get "hooked," by drugs, by code patching, or by "problem employees." Ultimately, implanting a more effective model is the most helpful intervention.

## 10.4 Helpful Hints and Suggestions

• Pattern 1 and Pattern 2 people are frequently found accusing one another of being destructive. Programmers believe that managers can manage best by staying out of their way, while managers believe that programmers are trying to avoid responsibility. They would both benefit from the Helpful Model, which might remind them that Pattern 2 people are often trying bigger things than Pattern 1. Often, the Routine managers are trying to enlarge products that were initially developed in a Variable culture. This effort brings them up against the Size/ Complexity Dynamic, which may account for some of the "bizarre" things they try to inflict on programmers.

• Routine cultures, when done well, often create Variable environments within themselves to do things that they don't do well, such as small projects or projects requiring creative breakthroughs. These Pattern 1 environments may be individuals, teams, or third party developers. Rather than being accused of recognizing that Variable culture is "better," perhaps they should be congratulated for trying to be helpful—and for their understanding of the dynamics of software engineering. They are a good step along the way to a Steering culture, and ought to be encouraged.

• When buying software tools, ask the vendor to provide a size/risk graph showing their experience with a number of projects. If all problem sizes have a 100% chance of success, they're either ignorant, stupid, or totally lacking in scruples. Don't buy a tool from a fool, a mule, or a ghoul.

• If you ask Routine managers (or survey them) to draw size/risk curves for their organizations, you'll tend to get an overestimate of their prowess, because they don't *know* what's happening in their organization. Thus, again Pattern 2 may look on the surface as capable as Pattern 3. Ask them to put some data points on the graph and see how they correspond to their curves. If they can't supply data points, ask them why not.

• If you ask managers to create size/effort curves or size/risk curves, they may start an argument over which measure of "size" they ought to use. Don't let yourself get involved in such arguments. Apply the Principle of Addition and create a separate graph for each person who is willing to support their favorite measure with a little data-gathering effort. If they're not willing to gather data, politely ignore their arguments. You'll probably find that all the graphs look more or less alike. If not, you'll learn something very useful.

## 10.5 Summary

1. Our brains will never be big enough for our ambitions, so we'll always need thinking tools, such as size/effort graphs.

2. Size/effort graphs can be used to reason about the Size/Complexity Dynamic, such as when estimating a project or comparing the impact of two different technologies. Graphs, however—such as log-log graphs—can also distort or conceal the non-linear nature of the dynamic. We must learn to see the stable meaning through the variations in the data and the method of presentation.

3. Because of the Size/Complexity Dynamic, it's easy to write requirements that the most competent programmers cannot satisfy.

4. A single method or tool is seldom the best over the entire range of problem sizes. Size/effort graphs can help managers combine two methods into a composite pattern that adopts the best range for each one.

5. "The bottom line" doesn't dictate all technology choices. Managers are often willing to pay a lot on the bottom line to reduce the risk of failure. The size/risk graph can help in reasoning about these choices, especially when used in conjunction with the size/effort graph.

6. If you set out to change an organization, the first rule should be the one given to physicians by Hippocrates" "Do no harm."

7. We are all subject to the Size/Complexity Dynamic, so interactions intended to be helpful often wind up being irrelevant, or actually destructive. It's a good idea to assume that regardless of how it looks or sounds, everyone is trying to be helpful.

8. We can help most when we apply the The Principle of Addition to add more effective models to a person's repertoire.

## 10.6 Practice

1. Give an instance when you thought someone was being disruptive but it turned out they were only trying to be helpful. How did you discover their intention? How can you do it earlier next time?

2. Give an instance when someone thought you were being disruptive, when you were only trying to be helpful. What could you do next time to ensure that they know you're actually trying to be helpful?

3. Draw a size/risk curve for your own organization's culture? How big a problem can you solve in a satisfactory manner at least 50% of the time? At least 90% of the time? At least often enough to meet your customers' tolerance for risk?

# Chapter 11: Responses to Customer Demands

*"When printing stylized text (shadow or outline) in large point sizes on the ImageWriter LQ and the LaserWriter IIsc, some characters may not print. This problem only occurs with a Mac Plus, or SE, and varies depending on the application, font, font style and font size being used. When this happens, Apple recommends plain text." - from Apple Computer's Change Histories for Macintosh System 6.02*

You can often tell an organization is in crisis by the attitudes expressed towards their customers and other outsiders. A crisis organization is so entangled in its internal problems that it forgets its fundamental reason for existence. Up until now, we have considered the dynamics of the software organization as if it were a more-or-less *closed* system—which is the way many software organizations see themselves. In this chapter, we want to introduce a jolt of reality by relaxing that assumption, and seeing how outside influences contribute to instability of a development process.

## 11.1 Customers Can Be Dangerous To Your Health

In Chapter 3, we introduced the concept of "customer demands," and how they influenced the organization's need to move to new patterns (see, for example, Figure 3-1). Just what do we mean by customer demands, and how exactly do they press upon an organization's choice of pattern?

### 11.1.1 More customers increase the development load

You know your software development organization is in

258

trouble when you hear such complaints as,

"We have too many customers."

"If only our customers didn't bother us, we could have a great system."

"Why do they need all this stuff? We know what's best for them."

And, of course, these complaints are justified. If you think adding workers to a project is bad, think about what happens when you add *customers*. Figure 11-1 shows a natural dynamic underlying the trouble with customers. No two customers are identical, so each added customer potentially adds requirements, which increases the size of the system and invokes the Size/ Complexity Dynamic. This in itself would be a non-linear effect, but some of those added requirements don't just differ among customers—they conflict.

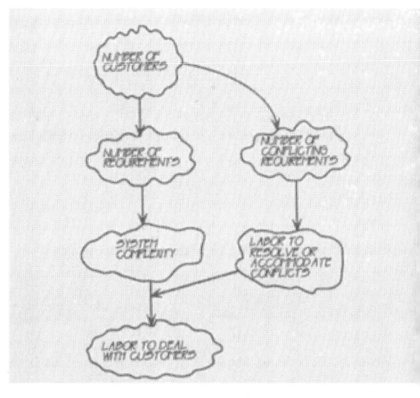

**Figure 11-1. As the number of customers increases, the development labor needed to deal with customer requirements grows non-linearly.**

Conflicting requirements added to the labor needed to build a system through one or more of the following:

• *labor to resolve the conflict*

• *labor to explain to explain why the resolution went one way and not the other*

• *labor to create and maintain multiple systems that satisfy everybody*

**11.1.2 More customers increase the maintenance load**

260

Even if you increase the number of customers on an existing product, without changing the way you do business, you may collapse your cultural pattern, as suggested in Figure 11-2.

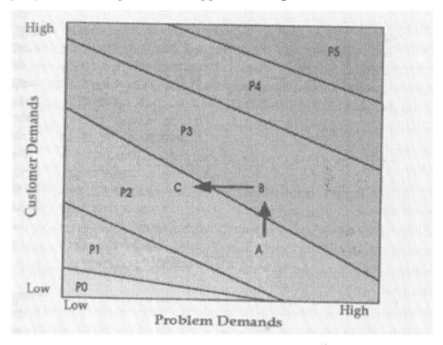

**Figure 11-2. Growth in number of customers can, by itself, push an organization into a new region requiring a new cultural pattern. This kind of growth usually takes place faster than an organization can change its culture, so the organization must take steps to reduce the effective number of customers, or else break down.**

This type of collapse has actually befallen several of our clients, as in the following case:

We were called in to consult with a software organization that had been an independent software vendor until acquired 8 months earlier by a much larger company known for its aggressive marketing. Their product, Zodiacal Business Forecasts (ZBF), was full of attractive features—on paper. Most of the features didn't work very well, a fact that was known to most of their 40 original customers. These customers had bought ZBF in the full knowledge that most features didn't work, in order to get the use of one or two other features that worked reasonably well. These customers weren't delighted with ZBF's present buggy condition, but they were getting value for money, and had never been misled about the condition of the product.

The same could not be said for the 110 new customers the parent organization brought into the ZBF fold in the first 6 months of aggressive marketing. Most of them had been led to believe that all features listed in the marketing documents were working as one would expect in a mature product. Moreover, many of them had been promised enhancements to meet their *real* needs.

When this wave of new customer demands hit the ZBF organization, it collapsed. And, just to make sure that it had no chance of recovery, the new management "helped meet the new customer demand" by tripling the size of the development staff. Two months later, we were approached by a desperate user group to see what we could do.

This example shows that the non-linear effects of customers are not confined to initial development activities. More customers for ZBF meant increased customer demands throughout the development organization because there were

- more field failures reported more quickly
- more pressure to repair these failures quickly
- more requests for new features
- more requests for changes to old features
- more interactions with customers
- more configurations to support
- more releases under maintenance

All these increase the amount of work to be done while reducing the resources available to do other work—a sort of Brooks's Law applied to customers. Added to this was the real Brooks's Law effect of tripling the number of developers in a few months, plus extra labor need to create a new working relationship with each new customer. These changes could not be handled by the existing culture, so either the culture had to be changed or the number of customers reduced. Later, we'll see how, because the culture couldn't be changed fast enough, ZBF set in motion a program of reducing the *effective* number of customers while they could get back on their feet.

### 11.1.3 Close contact with customers can be disruptive

If we imagine the software development organization as an organism, then the customers have many of the characteristics of *disease carriers.* If we get in too close contact with them, we can get "infected," and if we are "infected," we cannot do a good job of producing software. In order to regulate the system's output, the controller must keep the system healthy, and so must also deal with these "outside" forces (Figure 11-3).

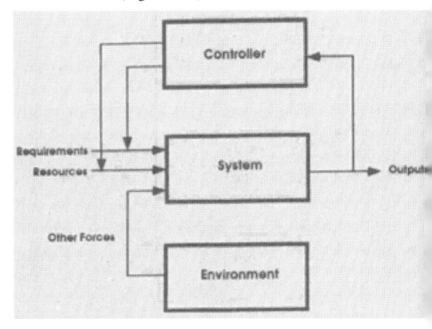

**Figure 11-3. The feedback model of a system can be elaborated by showing that part of the system is dedicated to regulating outside forces, such as disease organisms.**

### 11.1.4 You can be disruptive to your customers.

Of course, the customers can look at your software organization the same way, with equal justification. Perhaps we can improve the analogy by thinking of the customers as *mates.* Your organization needs intimate contact with them for survival of the species, but close contact may expose the organization to some terrible disease—or at least a common cold. Like mates, customers do not *intend* to cause diseases. It's in their best interest to have a healthy mate. The same goes for your development organization. If you make your customers sick, then you go out of business.

Figure 11-4 shows a more complete interpretation of the "mate" model, where the customer system needs the outputs of the software development system. To get these outputs, it supplies requirements to say what it needs and resources to empower the development system to produce them. In the process, it also supplies some "randomness," or "viruses," which are a potential threat to getting what it wants. It's not always easy for the customer system to know which inputs are which, primarily because many of the inputs serve more than one role.

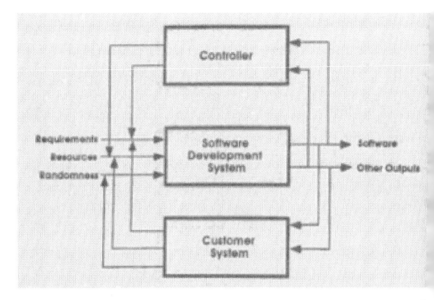

**Figure 11-4. The feedback model of a software development system can be elaborated with an interpretation of the customer's role as a supplier of external inputs. Some of these inputs are necessary requirements, but others are seen as random disturbances.**

Notice that in this view, the customer looks just like a controller, and, of course, it is. The customer, like any controller, is trying to control the software development system to get just what it wants. The customer's attempts to control will sometimes be in concert with the system's own controller, but sometimes the two controllers will be out of synchronization. In those cases, the customer organization is actually working against its own ultimate purposes, but doesn't know it. It's easy to see how that situation can contribute to instability, as in the case of the electric blanket.

### 11.1.5 What happens when you have many customers

The situation is even worse if we add yet another level of reality. The common cold can be caused by over 200 known viruses, and there are lots of other viruses that cause worse problems than colds. Figure 11-5 suggests the situation in which there is more than one customer. The development system *wants* multiple customers because it can obtain more resources from them, but in return it gets multiple requirements, some of which are in conflict, and lots of extra "randomness," as we saw in the ZBF case.

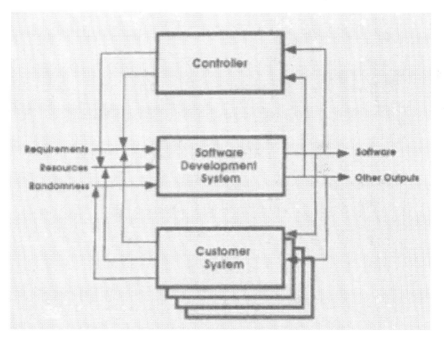

**Figure 11-5. When there are multiple customers, there are more potential resources, but there are also multiple requirements, which may conflict, and lots more randomness.**

## 11.2 The Cast of Outsiders

Customers are not the only dangerous "outsiders." There are so many outsiders who threaten the stability of software development that it is useful to lump them into several major categories.

### 11.2.1 Customers and users

Sometimes, it's helpful to distinguish customers from "users." users are anybody who is affected by the system. You may not need to satisfy all of them, as you do the customers, who have the "right" to define quality by giving you requirements. Even so, the users are out there interacting with the system, and that in itself will eventually produce some sort of extra requirements. At the very least, the users are experiencing failures. When these failures come back to your organization, they become become requirements about faults to locate and fix.

### 11.2.2 The marketing department

In development organizations that sell their products, we often find a *marketing department*. Marketing is not the customer of the development department, but is a *surrogate* that *represents* the customer, sometimes well and sometimes badly. If you satisfy the customers, you don't really have to satisfy marketing, but if you don't trust marketing, then you have a problem.

If customers are like disease carriers, then marketing is like a hypodermic injection of medicine. We create a marketing function to stand between the disease carrier and the system, to reduce the flow of disturbances (Figure 11-6). "Marketing" in this sense may include a variety of functions, such as, developing product requirements, aiding the installation of new systems, training users, and servicing any problems that arise at the customer's location.

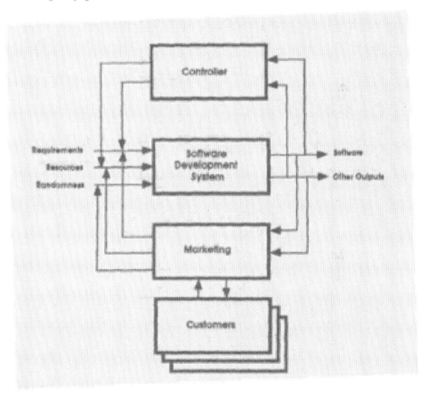

**Figure 11-6. The marketing department is created to stand between the customer population and the development organization—to filter inputs and outputs. In reducing the flow of disturbance, this role is helpful—but because it is closer to**

**the core of the development organization, it has great potential for harm.**

In return for this reduction of disturbances, however, we put another group of people—the marketing staff—nearer the core of the system, under the skin ("hypo-dermic") as it were. Because of this position of the marketing department, *their* disturbances bypass all other defenses. There are not so many of them, but each one is harder to deal with because they are already "inside." The effect of these people wandering around among the development staff is like a strong medicine wandering inside your body. They act faster, and they act undiluted. You may get "side-effects" that are worse than the original disease. That's why the marketing organization—like any medicine—can so easily stop being a solution and start being a problem.

### *11.2.3 Other surrogates*

Marketing departments aren't the only surrogates. Even when the product is not sold, but developed internally, organizations create the position of *customer liaison* to stand between developer and customer. The effect of all such surrogates is to change the actual number of customers to an "effective number"—the number with which the development organization has to deal (Figure 11-7).

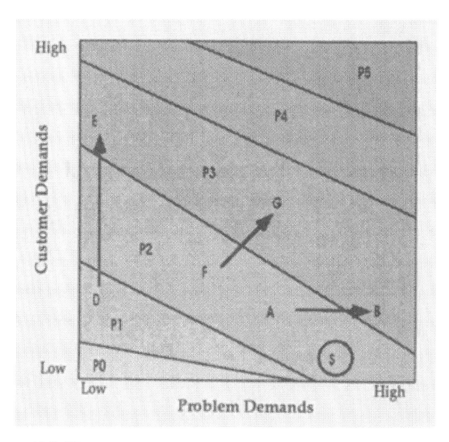

**Figure 11-7. The surrogate, if acting effectively, reduces the effective number of customers, thus reducing the non-linear effects of the number of customers.**

Another common surrogate is the *customer service department*, which is sometimes considered part of marketing, sometimes part of development, and sometimes independent. An independent customer service function serves the filtering function best, if it truly cannot be co-opted by development or marketing. This is the approach we used at ZBF, although we met great

271

resistance from the old-time developers who wanted to give the customers "personal service," as they had in "the good old days." The initial result was a reduction in the amount of interference from the new customers, but it took more than a year and a complete change in the phone system before even half of the old customers stopped calling the developers directly.

### 11.2.4 Programmers as self-appointed user surrogates

Programmers appoint themselves as user surrogates. In that sense, they are "inside-outsiders." If they're not satisfied, they have the power to stop the system from working, just like the customers —but faster. If marketing is like a hypodermic injection of medicine, programmers are even worse—like an injection of viruses that migrates directly to the insides of cells. From there, they can do awesome things—awesome in their creativity or awesome in their destructiveness, or both. It is this destructive potential that so strongly motivates Routine managers to get rid of all traces of Variable culture.

Paradoxically, programmers are not likely to act as customer or user surrogates in a Variable culture because of the close, one-to-one relationship that often exists between programmer and customer. If Variable programmers wonder what the customers want, they ask. The more customers they have, however, the more likely they are to make decisions for customers on the fly, whether authorized or not.

One of the marks of an unstable organization is how frequently the programmers are making unauthorized, and often unnoticed, decisions about what the customer really wants. Making decisions for customers is a tempting short-cut when the pressure mounts. You can almost hear the programmers muttering:

"They'll love this neat trick."

"They'd never want to do that anyway."

"This will be much clearer, especially to the smart ones."

"If they don't like this feature, they don't deserve it."

And sometimes, even most of the time, the programmers are right. But what about when they are not? Then, the more programmers you have, the more potentially dangerous customer surrogates you have.

### 11.2.5 Testers as official and unofficial surrogates

Testers, of course, are official surrogates of the customers, attempting to faithfully replicate customer use of a system before the customers have to suffer from its slings and arrows. If effective in this role, they can dampen the effects of increased numbers of customers, but being closer to the developers than the customers, they often fail to act as effective surrogates. Rather than annoy a developer, they will all too easily agree with the developer who argues, "What customer in their right mind would want to do that?"

Unofficially, then, they are incessantly making implicit

decisions about what customers would and wouldn't do. This implicit decision making is characteristic of Pattern 2 organizations, and tends to thwart the best laid testing plans.

### 11.2.6 Other unplanned surrogates

Liaisons and customer service people are planned responses to increased customer demand, but outsiders may appoint themselves customer surrogates, just as the programmers do from the inside—to be helpful. One customer may speak—or claim to speak—for a group of customers. A so-called "user group" is a surrogate for a group of customers. The ladies and gentlemen of the press may take it upon themselves to act "on behalf of" a group of users—or even potential users. And, I shudder to think of it, some branch of the government may decide that only they know what's best for the users.

Each of these surrogates can gather information that would be difficult to obtain elsewhere, and can, like marketing, provide filtering factors for excessive amounts of feedback. Yet they can also provide additional doses of trouble for the unstable organization to handle. From the dynamic point of view, the critical questions about any outsider, surrogate or otherwise, are these:

• Where do they interact with the system—close in or far away?

• With what force, or volume, do they interact?

• With what frequency do they appear?

Let's examine a few important "attacks," keeping in mind that they probably were intended to be helpful.

## 11.3 Interactions With Customers

As the number of customers increases, the most obvious dynamical change is that the number of interactions with customers must change. How does the number of interactions grow, and how does this growth affect the productivity and quality of the organization?

### 11.3.1 The dynamics of interruption

An hour of work is not an hour of work if you are interrupted during the hour. DeMarco and Lister studied the effect of interrupt-free time on productivity. They cite a metric

E-factor = Uninterrupted Hours / Body-Present Hours

They recorded a range of E-factors in their coding experiments from 0.10 to 0.38. The people in the first instance need 3.8 times as many body-present hours to accomplish the same work as those in the second instance ( p63ff).

This is a very approximate measure of the effect of interruptions. A more precise way of looking at this information is to consider the lasting effect of an interruption. DeMarco and Lister introduce the concept of "reimmersion time" :

"If the average incoming phone call takes five minutes and your reimmersion time is fifteen minutes, the total cost of that call in flow time (work time) lost is twenty minutes. A dozen phone calls use up half a day. A dozen other interruptions and the rest of the work day is gone. This is what guarantees, 'You never get anything done around here between 9 and 5.'" (p63)

### 11.3.2. Interrupted meetings

Of course, interruptions don't always come when we're working alone. DeMarco and Lister cite (p62) IBM's Santa Teresa study as showing that software developers spend 30% of their time working alone, 50% working with one other person, and 20% working with 2 or more others.

How does interruption affect the working together times? We observe that reimmersion time is greater the more people in the group that is interrupted. If, for instance, a meeting of seven people is interrupted for one person to take an emergency call, the other six people scatter out of the meeting room to attend to various tasks. The meeting then stays interrupted until the *last* of the seven returns, which can be a long time. These two factors create a non-linear effect of number of people on wasted time, as shown in Figure 11-8.

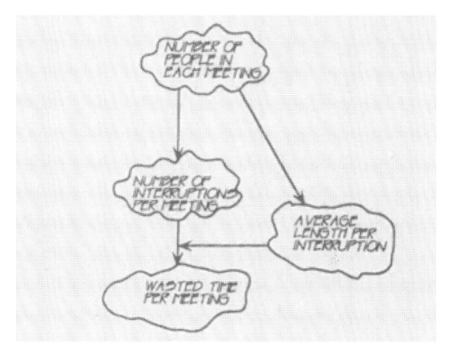

**Figure 11-8. The more people in the meeting, the more interruptions and the longer each interruption, so that wasted time is a non-linear effect of the size of the meeting.**

Once they are all together, there is still more time to get them all on the same track. Usually, this period is extended because some of the people "need" to discuss what happened when they were out of the room.

In one client, I kept track of a series of review meetings we were holding with seven people. Over six meetings, there were 13 interruptions where one of the people was called out of the room. The time between the call and the meeting getting back on track ranged from 13 minutes for 47 minutes, with an average of 21 minutes. (In the 47-minute interruption, two of the people never came back, but the meeting went on—in a fashion—without them after waiting 47 minutes.)

If this pattern is typical, and if the average meeting had seven people, then this client was wasting 21 x 7 = 147 work-minutes every time a meeting was interrupted. Some of that time was undoubtedly put to good use, but I would estimate a loss of two full hours of work-time for each meeting that was interrupted. At a burdened labor cost of $50 per hour, each interruption cost about $100. We created a sign asking:

IS THIS INTERRUPTION WORTH $100?

We hung the sign on the door of each review meeting. It seemed to have some effect.

### 11.3.3 Meeting size and frequency

McCue's observations are of one organization (IBM) doing one type of work. Our own observations show that these numbers vary from organization to organization, depending on a number of factors. Among these factors is the number of customers.

The number of customers affects both the frequency of meetings and their average size. We have observed that the number of meetings grows when the number of customers grows, but reaches a maximum at about 10-20 customers. Up to that point, increasing the number of customers has even greater non-linear effects on wasted time than suggested by the dynamic of Figure 11-8. In that case, the effects are better illustrated by Figure 11-9.

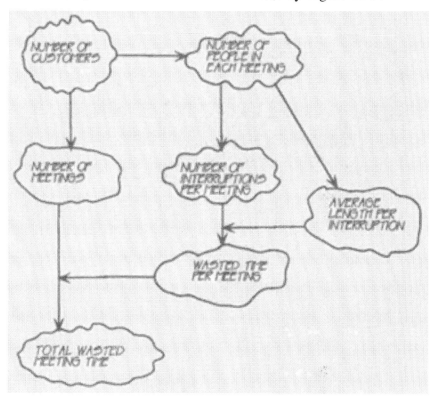

**Figure 11-9. The more customers, the more meetings and the larger those meetings are. These factors combine to create even more non-linearity in the amount of wasted time as the number of customers grows.**

Why doesn't the complexity grow after 10-20 customers? This curious pattern seems to arise from the customers' expectations. When a software organization serves a small number of customers, each customer organization seems to feel that it deserves to be given individual attention. This is the typical pattern

279

in several situations:

• an in-house application that serves a few customers because several departments have the same function to perform, like physical inventory

• a consortium arrangement, where the software developers serve a few organizations for cost savings, like the Bellcore organization which develops software for the former Bell operating companies

• a startup organization while it has its first few customers

In each of these cases, the people who decided to have one software package for several customers believed that their needs were similar. In practice, their needs, when considered in detail, are different, so the software organization must spend time meeting with each one to discover their exact needs, and to adapt the package to those individual needs.

When the number of customers grows much larger, however, it becomes physically impossible to serve each one's needs exactly. Moreover, most customers don't really *expect* that they will get the package modified to their exact needs. In any case, the software organization begins to treat customer needs *statistically*, so that they no longer need an ever-increasing number of customer meetings.

## 11.4 Configuration Support

More customers can mean more hardware configurations for the software to support, because marketing wants to reach everybody. What are some of the effects of multiple configurations?

### 11.4.1 Effects on test coverage and repair time

The number of configurations tends to grow exponentially over time, because a unique "configuration" is one that differs from other configurations in *any one component* that is touched by the software product. Thus, for example,

UGLI Software had one software product on a personal computer supported 15 different CPUs (some of which were "IBM compatibles" but were in fact slightly different from the IBM original), 21 different printers, 16 different disk drives, and 4 different networks. This led to 15 x 21 x 16 x 4 = 20,160 different configurations, without counting different software that the word processor had to work with.

Of course, not all these configurations could be tested. Though most of them worked quite well, not a day would pass without some customer calling UGLI technical service department with a problem on a configuration they'd never seen before. And, when such customers did call, UGLI often couldn't reproduce the configurations in their test lab. They had to work on locating the problem without having the actual hardware configuration that the customer was using. Even when they could reproduce them, the setup time added to the time to fix the errors.

Different configurations mean that test coverage is less thorough. This means that there will be more faults to repair. But different configurations means that each repair takes longer, but also that each single repair is a multiple repair—the multiplier being perhaps as great as the number of configurations supported. Therefore, the number of repairs can be much greater than the number of faults in the software, and also grows non-linearly with the number of customers. Total repair time, of course, is total repairs multiplied by the time per repair. The total effect is shown in Figure 11-10.

Obviously, in practice, any software culture that produces high numbers of faults could never keep up with all the potential configurations. They are thus forced either to change their culture or lower their support level for configurations. They generally choose the latter, for reasons that will become obvious in the analysis of the following section.

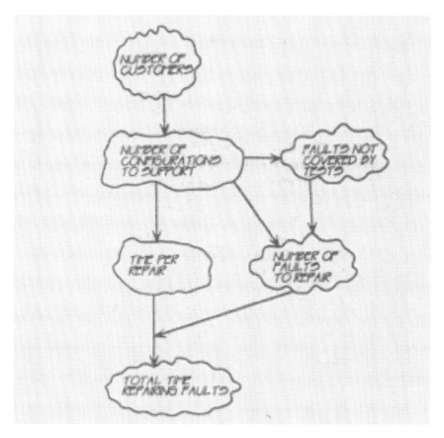

**Figure 11- 10. A large number of customers has a non-linear effect on the amount of time spent repairing faults, because of the larger number of potential configurations.**

*11.4.2 Analyzing the testing situation externally—an Apple example*

The Apple quote at the beginning of this chapter is a typical example of what happens when any developer attempts to continue to support multiple feature combinations on multiple hardware configurations. I know the story of the Apple release 6.02 only as a devoted Macintosh user, not as an insider, so it makes a good example of analyzing a situation externally.

At the time of this System release, if I'm counting correctly, Apple was supporting 7 Macintosh CPUs, and 7 official Apple printers, for at least 49 different relevant hardware configurations. (People with non-Apple printers and CPU upgrades presumably had already learned to take their own chances on what would work and what wouldn't.)

On the software side, the problem is much worse. There is no limit to the number of fonts, but just taking fonts that Apple released with their printers, you had perhaps 10 to support. The "style" menu offers 7 options besides "plain"—bold, italic, underline, outline, shadow, condensed, and extended. The first five of these can be used in any combination, which makes 32 different combinations, of which "plain" is only one instance. Any of these can be normal, condensed, or extended, which means there are 3x32=96 styles for each font. Font size can be just about anything —I have used from 4 point to 72 point—but let's say we consider 8 to be a typical number shown on the font menu. Not even worrying about what might happen if you superscripted or subscripted a 72 point Zapf Chancery condensed italic shadow font, Apple has to test 10x96x8=7680 font combinations.

But the memo states that the results vary "depending on the application." There are hundreds of Macintosh applications, but suppose that Apple only tested for the top 100. They would now

284

have 100 applications, times 49 hardware configurations, time 7680 font combinations, for a grand total of 37,632,000 configurations to test for proper printing. Assume that with highly automated testing techniques Apple could test one configuration in the amount of time it took to print a page. Then, with the seven different printers working simultaneously, it would require over 5 years to test each of these configurations. If 10 tests could be printed on a page, then the output paper would stack about as high as a 120 story building—and somebody would have to check each paper carefully to see which characters did not print.

What this analysis shows is that neither Apple nor anyone else in their situation can actually expect to test all the configurations they supposedly "support." As a result, they can expect a continuing stream of complaints from their customers who try "bizarre" combinations of features. And, indeed, I myself found a certified hardware error in my LaserWriter Plus when trying to print expanded, outline Times font in a header. It worked swell on the first page, but not on the second. Perhaps they only tested the first page. Or only tested footers, and didn't test headers at all. Would you be surprised?

## 11.5 Releases

This Apple problem appeared in "release 6.02" of the system software. A "release" is a point at which a piece of work passes from one group to another. More specifically, a software release takes place when the work actually begins to be used for some productive work. The 6.02 means (probably) that this was the second "minor" revision of the sixth major release. We can't be sure because marketing departments play tricks with release numbers so that their software development culture doesn't look quite so shabby.

### 11.5.1 Pre- and post-release dynamics

The release concept is critical to software quality dynamics because at the moment of release, the dynamical structure changes. For instance,

• More than one version of the software now exists, and each version must be accounted for at all times. You are not really working with one system, but with N systems, which threatens to multiply the workload by N right off the bat. And sometimes N can be very large.

• Errors flow into the development organization at a much faster rate, in a much less organized fashion, because there are more people finding errors.

• The urgency of correcting errors is much greater, because once the product is in real use, it must usually continue in use— uninterrupted. Thus, part of the development organization is now driven by an external clock—perhaps many external clocks—

rather than being largely in control of its own pace.

• The cost of an incorrect change is much greater, sometimes millions of times greater, because effects are no longer confined to the development organization's boundaries. Costs are incurred in the customer's own business, and more than one business has been driven into bankruptcy by released errors. Only software companies fail because of unreleased errors.

### 11.5.2 Multiple versions

With only a single customer, the "release concept" doesn't really apply, as there is only one physical copy of the software in use, which effectively defines the current state. You may, of course, have another version in ongoing development. With more customers, you need releases, or else you would have to maintain as many versions of the system as there are customers. If you have discrete release points, in theory there will be only as many versions to maintain as there are active releases, plus those releases that are in process internally.

In practice, more customers means more versions than the release concept would imply. If a release hits a major customer and doesn't work, the software organization will often send a patch to that customer. Different customers soon have different collections of patches, each one amounting to a somewhat different release. Again, this effect is most pronounced with a moderate numbers of customers, and tends to disappear when you have enough customers to treat them statistically, with no special favors.

More releases in operation at any given time means more trouble with repairs, because each repair must work with every release in use. In theory, this means that every repair has to be tested against every release, but under pressure, this conservative approach may be short cut. This increases the chances of introducing new errors.

More customers means that people will be installing the releases at many different times, so that repairs may accumulate, and then not be applied in the right order, or some not applied at all. This adds to the complexity of understanding failure reports.

Once an item—a single patch or a whole system—is released to the customers, it follows a different dynamic than an internal item. Customers start using the item to do their work, so if it fails, the urgency to repair is much greater than for a similar failure inside the development organization.

Moreover, failures in the development cycle tend to occur at times when the organization is prepared for failures, with people dedicated to fixing them and getting on with the development. Failures after release to many customers come in on an almost continuous basis, interrupting all other work at any stage.

### 11.5.3 Release frequency
Management often tries to cut down on the failure load by

slowing down the repair releases, but this means that distribution time gets longer, and so the same failure is reported more often. On the other hand, as the number of customers increases, the pressure to release more frequently increases, which tends to balance the pressure to make release time longer. Perhaps that is why we often find software products in mature organizations released exactly twice a year, regardless of the application, the number of customers, or any other factor. If release frequency varies a great deal from twice a year, it may be a sign of instability, and suggests that deeper examination of the dynamics would be profitable.

### 11.6. Helpful Hints and Suggestions

• The liaison is supposed to represent the customer to the developers and the developers to the customers, filtering demands from each, and reducing the effective numbers. Often, the liaisons get co-opted by one side or the other, whereupon they serve as amplifiers—rather than filters—of disturbance.

• There is a dynamic of the "difficulty of satisfying" customers versus the number of customers. Factors in this dynamic include the customers' expectations of getting all their requirements satisfied, the developer's standards for satisfying customers, and the difficulty of satisfying multiple requirements. As the number of customers goes up, after a certain point most customers no longer expect to have all their wishes satisfied.

Similarly, the developers don't imagine that they can satisfy each of 100,000 customers exact requirements.

The result is a hump-backed curve, which my own observations indicate usually peaks at around 9 customers. This is the kind of thing you get when a consortium of single customers decides to get together and share work to save development costs. Each expects to get its own way in everything because the price they are paying is still much bigger than a software product price would be.

• As the number of customers grows even further, the developers first try to satisfy all of them, but eventually are unable to do this. In self-protection they start to assign "importance" to different customers, perhaps on the basis of how much they are paying, or perhaps on how nice (or nasty) they are in dealing with the developers. At some size, any individual customer is written off with a shrug of the shoulders and the remark, "You can't satisfy every bizarre request."

• Fred Brooks was the first to write about the difference between a program and a program product. A product must have more function and also be "bulletproof," so the amount of work goes up non-linearly. Managers who have successful programs often get tempted to make them into products, without realizing this dynamic, let alone the dynamic of releases and of combinatoric configurations.

## 11.7. Summary

1. The relationship with customers is the second important factor driving organizations to particular software cultural patterns.

2. Simply increasing the number of customers can wreak vast changes on an organization, such as

- increasing the development load
- increasing the maintenance load
- disrupting the pattern of development work

3. On the other hand, a software development organization can be extremely disruptive to its customers. That's why customers try to be controllers of the software development organization, leading to a situation of multiple controllers. The more controllers, the more "randomness" there appears to the other controllers.

4. The cast of outsiders who may influence software development is enormous, including such roles as

- customers and users
- the marketing department
- other surrogates
- programmers as self-appointed user surrogates
- testers as official and unofficial surrogates
- other unplanned surrogates

5. Many of these outsider roles are planned as attempts to reduce the effective number of customers.

6. Because some of the surrogates are much more intimate with the development system, they may negate their reduction of the effective number of customers with the force and frequency of their interactions.

7. Interactions with customers are fraught with peril as the number of customers grows. Interruptions increase. Meetings increase in size and frequency. Time lost because of interrupted meetings increases. All of these increases are non-linear.

8. With more customers comes more configurations to support. More configurations means additional coding, more complex testing, less effective test coverage, and longer repair times.

9. Releases are needed whenever there are multiple customers. As soon as a product is released to customers, it assumes an entirely different dynamic than when it was held in the shadow of the development organization.

10. Multiple versions of a software product complicate maintenance enormously, but more customers means more versions, whether official or unofficial. Frequent releases complicate the development/maintenance process, but so do infrequent releases, so that almost all software cultures tend to stabilize releases at around two per year.

## 11.8. Practice

1. Draw a diagram of effects, similar to the Brooks's Law diagram, showing how increasing the number of customers affects a development organization. Are there any self-limiting feedback loops in your diagram?

2. What forces affect the identification of a customer service organization with the customers? What forces affect their identification with the developers? Can you diagram these forces?

3. Explain why it's usually faster to reduce the effective number of customers than to change the culture of a development organization.

4. Propose a set of guidelines that could reduce the effect of number of customers on meeting size and frequency.

5. Propose a set of guidelines that could reduce the effect of the size of meetings on the amount of time wasted. What difficulties do you foresee in applying these guidelines in your own organization?

# Appendix A: The Diagram of Effects

One of the important skills of Steering managers is the ability to reason about non-linear systems. One of the favorite tools for thinking about non-linear systems is the *diagram of effects* . Figure A-1 is an example of a diagram of effects showing some effects of management pressure to resolve software failures (STIs). We can use this diagram to explain the major notational conventions of the diagram of effects.

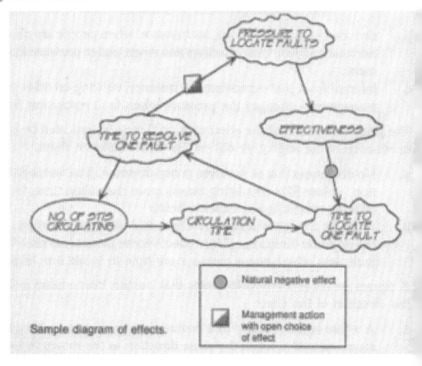

**Figure A-1. A diagram of effects.**

A diagram of effects consists primarily of nodes connected by arrows:

1. Each node stands for a measurable quantity, like circulation time, effectiveness, time to locate one fault, or pressure to locate faults. I use the "cloud" symbol rather than a circle or rectangle to remind us that nodes indicate *measurements*, not *things or processes* as in flow charts, data flow diagrams, and the like.

2. These cloud nodes may represent actual measurements, or they may represent conceptual measurements—things that could be measured, but are not measured at present. They may be too expensive to measure, or not worth the trouble, or just not happen to be measured yet. The important thing is that they *could* be measured—perhaps only approximately—if we were willing to pay the price.

3. When we wish to indicate an actual measurement currently being made, we use a very regular, elliptical "cloud," as we see for "number of STIs circulating." Most of the time, however, we'll use effects diagrams for *conceptual*—rather than mathematical— analysis, so most of the clouds will be appropriately rough.

4. An arrow from node A to node B indicates that quantity A has an *effect* on quantity B. We may actually know the effect in one of three ways:

   a. We have a mathematical formula for the effect, as in

   time to locate one fault = circulation time + other factors

   b. The effect is deduced from observations. For instance,

we've seen people get nervous and lose their effectiveness when under pressure from management.

c. The effect may be inferred from past experience. For instance, we've noticed on other projects how management changes the pressure when fault resolution time changes.

5. The general direction of the effect of A on B may be indicated by the presence or absence of the gray dot on the arrow between them.

a. No dot means that as A moves in one direction, B moves in the *same* direction. (*More* STIs circulating means *more* circulation time; *less* STIs circulating means *less* circulation time.)

b. A dot on the arrow means that as A moves in one direction, B moves in the *opposite* direction. (*More* effectiveness means *less* time to locate one fault; *less* effectiveness means *more* time to locate one fault.)

6. Squares on an effects line indicate that human intervention is determining the direction of the effect:

a. A white square means the human intervention is making the affected measurement move in the same direction to the movement of the cause (just as a plain arrow indicates a *natural* same direction).

b. A gray square means the human intervention is making the affected measurement move in the opposite direction to the movement of the cause (just as a gray dot indicates a *natural* opposite direction).

a. A white/gray square means the human intervention can make the affected measurement move in the same or the opposite direction to the movement of the cause, depending on the intervention. In this case, management can react to increased fault resolution time by either increasing or decreasing pressure to locate faults.

# Appendix B: The Software Engineering Cultural Patterns

In these volumes, we've made extensive use of the idea of software cultural patterns. For ease of reference, this appendix will summarize various aspects of those cultural patterns.

To my knowledge, Crosby was the first to apply the idea of cultural patterns to the study of industrial processes. Crosby discovered that the various processes that make up a technology don't merely occur in random combinations, but in coherent patterns.

In their article, "A Programming Process Study," Radice, et al. adapted Crosby's "stratification by quality" scheme to software development. In his book, *Managing the Software Process* , Watts Humphrey of the Software Engineering Institute (SEI) extended their work and identified five levels of "process maturity" through which a software development organization might grow.

Other software engineering observers quickly noted the usefulness of Humphrey's maturity levels. Bill Curtis, then of MCC, and now at SEI, proposed a "software human resource maturity model" with five levels.

I believe that each of these models represents points of view of the same phenomenon. Crosby named his five patterns based largely on the *management attitudes* to be found in each. The names used by SEI are more related to the *types of processes* found in each pattern, rather than to the attitudes of management, a la Crosby. Curtis made his classification on the basis of *the way people were treated* within the organization.

In my own work with software engineering organizations, I most often use the cultural view combined with Crosby's original focus on management, and on attitudes, but find each view useful at various times. The following summary incorporates material from each point of view.

**Pattern 0. Oblivious Process**

*Other Names:* Doesn't exist in Crosby, Humphrey, or Curtis models.

*Metaphor:* Walking: When you want to go somewhere, you just go.

*View of themselves:* "We don't even know that we're performing a process."

*Management understanding and attitude:* No comprehension that quality is a management issue.

*Problem handling:* Problems are suffered in silence.

*Summation of quality position:* "We don't have quality problems."

***When this pattern is successful:*** To succeed, the individuals need three conditions:

a. I'm solving my own problems.

b. Those problems aren't too big for what I know is technically possible.

c. I know what I want better than anyone else.

***Process results.*** Results depend totally on the individual. No records are kept, so we don't have measurements. Because the customer is the developer, delivery is always acceptable.

## Pattern 1: Variable Process

***Other Names:***

Crosby: ======Uncertainty Stage
Humphrey: ======Initial Process
Curtis:============Herded

***View of themselves:*** "We do whatever we feel like at the moment."

***Metaphor:*** Riding A Horse: When you want to go somewhere, you saddle up and ride ... if the horse cooperates.

***Management understanding and attitude:*** No comprehension of quality as a management tool.

***Problem handling:*** Problems are fought with inadequate definition and no resolution—plus lots of yelling and accusations.

***Summation of quality position:*** "We don't know why we have quality problems."

***When this pattern is successful:*** To succeed, the individuals (or teams) need three conditions:

a. I have great rapport with my customer.
b. I'm a competent professional individual.
c. Customer's problem isn't too big for me.

***Process results:*** The work is generally one-on-one, customer and developer. Quality is measured internally by "it works," externally by relationship quality. Emotion, personal relations, and mysticism drive everything. There is no consistent design, randomly structured code, errors removed by haphazard testing. Some of the work is excellent, some is bizarre—all depending on the individual.

## Pattern 2: Routine Process

***Other Names:***

Crosby: Awakening Stage
Humphrey: Repeatable Process
Curtis: Managed

***View of themselves:*** "We follow our routines (except when we lose our nerve)."

***Metaphor:*** A train: Large capacity and very efficient ... if you go where tracks are. Helpless when off the tracks.

***Management understanding and attitude:*** Recognize that quality management may be of value, but unwilling to provide money or time to make it all happen.

*Problem handling:* Teams are set up to handle major problems. Long range solutions are not solicited.

*Summation of quality position:* "Is it absolutely necessary to have problems with quality?"

*When this pattern is successful:* To succeed, these organizations need four conditions:

a. The problem is bigger than one small team can handle.
b. The problem is not too big for our routine process.
c. The developers conform to our routine process.
d. We don't run into anything too exceptional.

*Process results:* The Routine organization has procedures to coordinate efforts—which it follows, though often in name only. Statistics on past performance are used not change, but to prove that they are doing everything in the only reasonable way. Quality is measured internally by numbers of "bugs." You generally find bottom up design, semi-structured code, with errors removed by testing and fixing. They have many successes, but a few very large failures.

## Pattern 3: Steering Process

*Other Names:*

Crosby: Enlightenment Stage
Humphrey: Defined Process
Curtis: Tailored

*View of themselves:* "We choose among our routines based on the results they produce."

*Metaphor:* A van: A large choice of destinations, but must generally stay on mapped roads, and must be steered to stay on road.

*Management understanding and attitude:* Through our quality program, we learn more about quality management, and become more supportive and helpful.

*Problem handling:* Problems are faced openly and resolved in an orderly way.

*Summation of quality position:* "Through commitment and quality improvement, we are identifying and resolving our problems."

*When this pattern is successful:* To succeed, these organizations need four conditions:

a. The problem is big enough that a simple routine won't work.

b. Our managers can negotiate with the external environment.

c. We don't accept arbitrary schedules and constraints.

d. We are challenged, but not excessively.

*Process results:* They have procedures, always well understood, but not always well-defined in writing, and which are followed even in crisis. Quality is measured by user response, but

303

not systematically. Some measuring is done, but everybody debates which measurements are meaningful. You typically find top down design, structured code, design and code inspections, and incremental releases. The organization has consistent success, when it commits to undertake something.

## Pattern 4: Anticipating Process

*Other Names:*

> Crosby: Wisdom Stage
> Humphrey: Managed Process
> Curtis: Institutionalized

*View of themselves:* "We establish routines based on our past experience with them."

*Metaphor:* An airplane: Fast, reliable, and can go anywhere there's a field,... but requires large initial investment

*Management understanding and attitude:* Understand absolutes of quality management. Recognize their personal role in continuing emphasis.

*Problem handling:* Problems are identified early in their development. All functions are open to suggestion and improvement.

*Summation of quality position:* "Defect prevention is a routine part of our operation."

***When this pattern is successful:*** To succeed, these organizations meet three conditions:

    a. They have procedures, which they follow, and improve.

    b. Quality&cost measured (internally) by meaningful statistics.

    c. An explicit process group aids the process.

***Process results:*** We may find function-theoretic design, mathematical verification, and reliability measurement. They have consistent success on ambitious projects.

## Pattern 5: Congruent Process

***Other Names:***

    Crosby: Certainty Stage
    Humphrey: Optimizing Process
    Curtis: Optimized

***View of themselves:*** "Everyone is involved in improving everything all the time."

***Metaphor:*** The Starship Enterprise: Can go where no one has gone before, can carry anything, and beam it anywhere, ... but is science fiction.

***Management understanding and attitude:*** Consider quality management an essential part of the company system.

***Problem handling:*** Except in the most unusual cases, problems are prevented.

***Summation of quality position:*** "We know why we do not have quality problems."

***When this pattern is successful:*** To succeed, these organizations meet three conditions:

    a. They have procedures which it improves, continuously.

    b. All key process variables are identified and measured automatically.

    c. Customer satisfaction drives everything.

***Process results:*** All of the good things achievable by the other patterns, plus willingness to spend to reach next level of quality. Quality is measured by customer satisfaction and mean time to customer failure (10-100 years). Customers love the quality, and may bet their life on it. In some sense, Pattern 5 is like Pattern 0, totally responsive to the customer ... but is much better at what it does.

# WHAT TO READ NEXT?

You have been reading Volume 1 of the Quality Software Series. If you found this volume useful, you may wish to continue with the other volumes of this series. You may find the entire series published a number of places, including the Kindle Store:

http://www.amazon.com/-/e/B000AP8TZ8

Below are book titles and links to web pages where you can sample Jerry's books at no cost and, if you'd like, buy them at low eBook prices in formats for all e-reading devices, or your computer.

## BOOKS FOR CONSULTANTS (AND OTHERS)

The Secrets of Consulting: A Guide to Giving and Getting Advice Successfully

More Secrets of Consulting: The Consultant's Tool Kit

Are Your Lights On?: How to Know What the Problem Really Is

Weinberg on Writing: The Fieldstone Method

Experiential Learning (3 volumes)

Agile Impressions

## THE QUALITY SOFTWARE SERIES

## THE SYSTEMS THINKING SERIES

## TECHNOLOGY/PSYCHOLOGY

# NOVELS: TECHNOLOGY LESSONS FRAMED IN FICTION ABOUT WOMEN OF POWER.

## SHORT FICTION: FUN LITTLE LESSONS.

Memorable little lessons a la Aesop.

Fabulous Feebles:

More Aesop-like lessons

~~~~~~~~~~~~~~~~~~~~~~~~~~~~~~~~~~~~~~~~~~~~~~~